On a Clear Night

On a Clear Night

Essays from the Heartland

Marnie O. Mamminga

WISCONSIN HISTORICAL SOCIETY PRESS

Published by the Wisconsin Historical Society Press
Publishers since 1855

The Wisconsin Historical Society helps people connect to the past by collecting, preserving, and sharing stories. Founded in 1846, the Society is one of the nation's finest historical institutions.

Order books by phone toll free: (888) 999-1669
Order books online: shop.wisconsinhistory.org
Join the Wisconsin Historical Society: wisconsinhistory.org/membership

Versions of these essays have previously appeared in the *Chicago Tribune, Chicago Tribune Magazine, The Christian Science Monitor, Daily Herald, Detroit Free Press Magazine, Lake Superior Magazine, Midwest Prairie Review, Reader's Digest,* and several *Chicken Soup for the Soul* books.

Printed in the United States of America
Cover design by Andrew J. Brozyna, AJB Design
Typesetting by Diana Boger
Cover photo: *As Night Slowly Fades Away* by Matthew Crowley
21 20 19 18 17   1 2 3 4 5

Library of Congress Cataloging-in-Publication Data
Names: Mamminga, Marnie O., author.
Title: On a clear night : essays from the heartland / Marnie O. Mamminga.
Description: [Madison] : Wisconsin Historical Society Press, [2017]
Identifiers: LCCN 2016047368 (print) | LCCN 2016058488 (e-book) | ISBN
    9780870208249 (paperback) | ISBN 9780870208256 (e-book) | ISBN
    9780870208256 (E-book)
Subjects: LCSH: Mamminga, Marnie O. | BISAC: BIOGRAPHY &
AUTOBIOGRAPHY /
    Personal Memoirs.
Classification: LCC PS3613.A5266 A6 2017 (print) | LCC PS3613.A5266 (e-book) |
    DDC 814/.6 [B] —dc23
LC record available at https://lccn.loc.gov/2016047368

For Lily, Amber, Joy, Elena, Ryan, Alice,
and those to come . . . may your journeys be lit
by the brightest stars in the Milky Way.

Contents

Preface

An evening star. A pale pink dusk.

Fireflies wing their way through the gloaming, the rhythmic flash of their golden lights inviting us to step out into the night. It promises to be a clear one.

And so we do.

Often, in the quiet of that gathering twilight, the moments of the day that brought us joy or sorrow or laughter begin to take on more significance.

Sometimes a deeper understanding of our day's experiences greets us boldly, like a full silver moon sliding up over a field or forest. Sometimes knowledge comes to us in smaller bursts, like the scattered flashes of fireflies. But most often, our awareness starts with just a stirring in the heart, like blossoming starlight.

For even though we were not seeking those moments, had not planned or anticipated them, they reflect who we are, where we've been, and, most importantly, what we were thinking. Pausing to ponder, we discover that those seemingly ordinary experiences often transcend into moments of unexpected grace.

My hope in writing these essays is that the light created when we share our similar everyday moments might dispel the shadows, illuminate our paths, and remind us that we are not alone, that we do not walk in darkness.

Come, let us look to the starlight together.

Oh, Youth!

Your children are not your children.
They are the sons and daughters of Life's longing for itself.
—KAHLIL GIBRAN

Marching Away

The day has a perfect pitch to it. Warm autumn light filters through treetops, back-dropped by a brilliant blue sky. Along Main Street, the distant rattles of drums and tuning horns are accented by a cacophony of conversation and laughter. Today is the annual high school homecoming parade.

All is about to begin.

Waiting for the shrill blast of the police siren to start the parade, I stand on a curb and watch the others gathered for the afternoon's festivities. Proud parents, local businesspeople escaping from work, grandparents in lawn chairs, and young mothers surrounded by small children line the parade route in eager anticipation.

"When's it going to start, Mama?" my five-year-old son asks impatiently.

"Soon," I reply. "Here, let's see how many red leaves we can find while we wait."

My two-year-old joins the search while the baby watches his brothers intently from his stroller.

I watch my three sons' sweet faces alight with eagerness. In a few short minutes, the football team will be rolling by in hay-wagon chariots, tossing candy as they go; shiny red fire engines will blast their sirens; and elaborate crepe paper floats filled with waving teenagers will cruise past.

Most fun of all will be the thrilling sound of the band. Colorful uniforms, flashy instruments, and joyful music will march toward us in one big mass.

"I hear them!" my oldest shouts.

"Here they come!" his little brother yells.

Squealing with laughter, they lean out over the precipice of their street-corner curb for a better look. Even the baby strains his little face to the sound of the approaching music.

In the distance, we hear the first snappy sounds of a Sousa beat. Muffled at first, the clear notes of the trumpets, steady cadence of the drums, and brash power of the trombones begin to emerge.

All of a sudden, the band is upon us. Leaping back to the safety of our curb, we watch as a blur of color and harmony sweeps by. Clear clarinets, high-pitched piccolos, and booming tubas pepper their notes into the air. Sailing by in their synchronized steps, the musicians flow steadily forward, sending their music aloft to dance in the autumn breeze.

We clap and clap with excitement. Then, just as suddenly as they appeared, they are gone. We watch with some sadness as they march on down the street, wishing the brief moment of their music could have lasted a little longer.

Twelve years later, the day has a perfect pitch to it once again. Warm autumn light filters through treetops back-dropped by a brilliant blue sky. Today is the annual high school homecoming parade. The shrill blast of a siren wakes me from my reverie. The parade is starting!

Today, I stand alone on the corner. I check my video camera to make sure all is set. In the distance, I can hear the muffled sound of mingling instruments and drums. My heart begins to pound with excitement.

Waving red and gold flags suddenly appear, mirage-like, on

the street's horizon. The notes of a familiar Sousa march begin to emerge.

Here comes the band!

Through the twirling flags, I spot the crisp white uniform of the senior drum major: my oldest son. Head held high, marching with smooth precision, he leads the band confidently down the street. Spotting me on the sidelines, he smiles brightly. I wave back, trying to hold the camera steady. Too soon, he is past.

Quickly I search for my middle son playing a trumpet in the fast clip of moving lines.

"Don't let me miss him," I pray, as they march steadily along.

There he is! Smack dab in the middle of the band, concentrating on the trumpet melody, he struts his freshman independence by wearing his golf uniform to show that musicians can be athletes, too. My camera lens catches him briefly as his line files by.

Spinning around, I see my youngest son's middle-school band approaching. I dash across the street for a better angle, just in time to catch him in the center of the front row. Music memorized, cavalier hat at a jaunty angle, his eyes twinkling, he proudly plies the slide of his trombone for the first time in a parade. For a second, he passes before the camera lens before he too moves out of view.

Not wanting the moment to end, I run clumsily down the street, video camera in hand, dodging spectators while trying to get another glimpse of them in their striding grace. But the marchers move too fast, and I cannot keep up.

Finally, I stop and catch my breath on a hilltop street corner. The flowing current of red-coated musicians marches down the hill toward the sparkling river that meanders through our town. The late afternoon sun flashes against their brassy instruments. Standing still, I listen as the echoing pulse of the band's song drifts sweetly away from me.

It is magical, this youthful music. Full of promise and hope, it fills the afternoon air with energy and beauty. The pull to follow is strong, but I hold back and let them go. In the dreamlike haze of the warm autumn light, I turn and head home, the gentle cadence of their music fading to a whisper.

Climbing into the Ring

"Who's better?" I asked my new husband of several weeks, "Cassius Clay or Muhammad Ali?"

He looked at me in wide-eyed terror. "You're kidding, aren't you?"

I shook my head meekly, wondering what was so wrong with my question.

"They're the same person!" he laughed, burying his head back into the sports page.

As a young bride, I was trying to acclimate myself to my husband's world of sports. Although my father and two brothers enjoyed sports, their interest was nothing compared with my husband's obsession. He watched all the games, knew all the statistics, analyzed all the coaches, and listened to all the sports talk shows on the radio. And he tried his best to draw me into his sporting world.

"Watch this replay!" he would shout from the TV room.

Dropping what I was doing, I'd dash through the house to catch sight of yet another spectacular catch, block, putt, run, or leap. Though I could recognize it as great stuff, the action didn't grab my attention like a good book, a long walk, stars on a clear night, or a beautiful piece of art on a museum wall.

Even when I joined my husband on an occasional sports outing, I found myself paying more attention to the people than the score, the cool breeze than the play, the peanuts than the pop-up.

As our marriage moved through the game plan of life, we had three sons. Unwittingly, I had produced the perfect team for a pickup game: pitcher, catcher, and batter. While my friends with daughters got all dolled up for outings of lunch and shopping, I threw on jeans for hours of fielding, refereeing, and yelling "RUN! You can make it!"

"Aren't you just a little bit disappointed you don't have a girl?" friends often asked.

"Not at all," I answered truthfully.

"Well, there's a special place in heaven for mothers of three boys," they replied, quoting from a popular parenting guide.

Pity is not part of my playbook.

As each son grew and took his section of the sports page at the breakfast table, I refused to sit on the sidelines. So what if I didn't have long hair to braid, sweet dresses to iron, or ballet shoes to polish? I wasn't going to be left in the dugout. I could be the ball girl or I could step up to bat.

In short order, I became one of the boys. I pitched. I putted. I fished. And a whole new world opened up to me. Activities I never would have chosen turned into wondrous adventures.

As pitcher for the neighborhood pickup game, I discovered the joy of watching a well-hit ball soar off a bat and into the sky, as well as the earthy smell of trampled grass on a hot summer's afternoon.

As chauffeur to the putting green, I marveled at the precision needed to nail a four-foot putt, as well as the birdsong that serenaded us from a nearby oak tree.

As threader of the worms, I experienced the excitement of a fish tugging on my line, as well as the shade-shifting brilliance of a setting sun.

Just about the time I grew accustomed to these activities, my boys moved into their teenage years, and I found my middle-aged self thrown into a whole new realm of challenges. Because I was often involved in transporting the guys, I decided there was no point in just sitting and waiting for them to finish. Against my better judgment, I joined in the action.

I spent hours on an overcast day climbing up a forty-foot pine tree, swinging from a rope, and yelling "Tarzan!" before plunging into the cold waters of a Northwoods lake.

I rode the fastest, steepest roller coasters at a theme park, screaming my head off, amazed that I allowed my body to be put in such a precarious situation.

I attended years of baseball conventions, running with a mob of fans for autographs of players I didn't even know. (I can beg with the best of 'em.)

I found myself at the top of a snow-covered mountain peak—a novice skier on too steep a slope—simply because my sons knew I would like the view.

"Go for it, Mom!" they said. "You can do it!"

And I did.

The highlights of my sporting career occurred, however, when my sons crossed over into my playing field. I knew I'd scored when my eighteen-year-old returned from the city and described the personal tour of the art museum he'd given his friends, when my sixteen-year-old discussed the contrasting novels of a popular author, when my thirteen-year-old spotted sparkling Orion in the velvety darkness of the sky and announced that it was his favorite constellation.

Hey, these guys even do lunch.

As we rode home from dropping my oldest son off for his freshman year at college, my younger sons and husband started a game of sports trivia.

"Name three pro basketball teams that don't end in *S*."

"Who holds the record for most home runs by a catcher?"

I listened vaguely as I watched the silver headlights of farmers' tractors glide down rows of moonlit cornfields. Breathing in the sweet scent of the late summer harvest, I noticed a sudden lull in their questioning. I seized the moment.

"Who was better," I asked, "Muhammad Ali or Cassius Clay?"

Stunned silence.

"Muhammad Ali?" answered one son.

"Cassius Clay?" guessed the other.

Their father burst out laughing. "They're the same person," he explained.

"Hey, that's a really cool trick question, Mom!" said one son.

"Let's try it on Billy and Greg when we get home," said the other.

Twenty-five years later, I have finally redeemed myself.

Just don't ask me the score.

Going to the Dance

The spring night is cool and rainy. My kid is hot and sweaty. It's the eighth-grade graduation dinner dance, and adolescent anxieties are running high. As I walk down the upstairs hallway to see if my fourteen-year-old son is ready to go, I am enveloped in the strong scent of cologne that wafts from his room.

"Do you think this tie goes with these pants?" he asks nervously.

He is dressed in his sixteen-year-old brother's clothes. Rather than wear his own attire for this special occasion, he banks on his big brother's tried and tested "coolness." I glance at his pant cuffs sweeping the floor, his tucked-in shirt hanging loose and baggy over his belt, and his brother's suede loafers ready to slide off his feet.

"The tie looks good," I say. "It's a perfect match."

With only a few minutes until blastoff, there's no point in starting over. If he's satisfied, then so am I. Time to go.

Heading off to his date's house for group pictures, I use this car-confined moment to remind him about good manners. He nods absently. His nervousness over this first formal event has taken his mind elsewhere.

As we park the car in his date's driveway, he whispers his own parting advice: "Mom, don't take too many pictures."

I get the message. Don't talk too much. Don't laugh too loudly. Basically, don't do anything to embarrass him in front of his friends.

My son's "date" is a longtime friend that he has known since first grade. Fresh from the beauty parlor, she is near tears because she thinks her hair is a disaster. Admiring her pretty dress, my son says she looks just fine. He's obviously paid close attention to his father's finesse with his mother over the years. I'm proud of him.

Chatting and laughing amicably, the gathered parents direct the photography session like a Hollywood shoot, snapping off rolls of film. I am a muted mom, muffling my chuckles and taking only four pictures. My son slides me a secret smile. He's proud of me.

Like a gaggle of giggling geese, the adolescents finally head out to the waiting van. Awkwardly, they debate where to sit. The end result is girls in front, boys in back. With quick and casual waves that belie the bittersweet beating of our hearts, we send our babies off to their first dance.

Three hours later, I'm back on the scene as pickup chauffeur. By this time, the dates have split up, the girls heading off to a sleepover. I watch as dozens of teenagers stream euphorically from the banquet hall. Teachers grin broadly as they wave goodbye to their charges. I overhear one remark to another, "Three hours is *way too long!*"

"How was it?" I ask as four hot, sweaty neighborhood buddies pile into my van.

"Too short!" they answer in unison.

"I wish it had lasted at *least* another hour!"

"It was so awesome!"

"Even the food was good!"

The combination of their animated conversation and body heat immediately steams up the car. Though the night is cool, I roll all the car windows halfway down. The boys think it is so they can wave and holler goodbye to their friends, which they do with great gusto.

"Who did you and your dates sit with for dinner?" I ask.

"Oh, we just ate with the guys," answers my son.

"You didn't eat with the girls?" I ask in amazement.

"Naw, we all split up as soon as we got there," he says. "Our dates wanted to talk to the other girls, so we guys just sat down."

So much for the seriousness of an eighth-grade first date. Nevertheless, the mention of the girls brings on a sudden moment of quiet reflection.

"The girls were, well, they were something else!" muses one.

"They were awesome!" says another.

"They looked, like, so different!" ponders the third.

"Yeah, they were . . . *really pretty!*" gushes the fourth.

Having seen these same girls at eight o'clock on school mornings when I drop my son off at school, I can understand the boys' surprise. Dressed in blue jeans and baggy flannel shirts, the girls, like the boys, come dressed for school in casual comfort.

For their first dance, however, the girls pulled out all the stops. Pretty necklines, feminine dresses, heels, makeup, jewelry, beauty parlor hair, the works. The eighth-grade boys are delightfully dazed.

"Did you dance?" I ask.

"Yeah, but was I ever nervous!" says one.

"I didn't have a clue what I was doing!" admits another.

"I've never even danced before!" confides a third.

"I just went out on the floor and started dancing," says the fourth. "I think by the end of the dance I was actually pretty good!"

With good food, beautiful girls, and no embarrassing moments on the dance floor, how could the evening have been more perfect?

"You know," says one, thoughtfully, "after all that dancing, I don't even think I smell too bad!"

"I just checked," says another. "My deodorant is still working!"

"I sprayed cologne all over my clothes before I left, just in case!" admits a third.

"I even put some in my shoes!" says the fourth.

Laughter rocks the car. I lower the windows all the way. Exhilarating, crisp spring air blows across my face. Happy, octave-changing voices float like music out into the night. As I drive my nest of fledglings home, I savor their joyful spirit in the midst of one of life's transitions.

With humor and honesty, they have gingerly taken their first awkward steps across the dance floor from boys to young men.

Looking out the windshield, I notice the clouds have cleared, and sparkling stars grace the sky. A beautiful ovation for an evening that smells of sweet success.

Driving Lessons

"Slow down! Slow down! Slow down!" my father yells, a distinct edge of panic in his voice.

As a novice fifteen-year-old driver, I am trying to downshift around a curve on a gravel country road and immediately respond to the yelling by hitting the brake. This action sends the car sliding, kills the engine, and jerks us to an abrupt halt. We sit in surprised silence as a cloud of fine dust sifts slowly down upon the car. I wait for an angry reprimand, but instead, my father takes a deep breath and calmly suggests I restart the engine. The driving lesson resumes.

That was thirty years ago. My father is gone and I am now the parent of three teenagers. What was his secret to remaining calm, time and time again, with his own brood of five kids? Struggling for that patience on a daily basis, I wish he were here to give me the answer.

Today, I am the parent scheduled for the road test. I click on my seat belt and watch as my own fifteen-year-old son climbs joyfully behind the steering wheel.

"This is so cool!" he says.

"Have you got your permit?" I ask.

"Of course," he says, waving it before my eyes. "Do you realize, Mom, that I'm the only one in my class who has never driven before?"

"Well, that makes you the only one who didn't break the law," I say.

"No," he says, "that makes me the only dork who doesn't know how to drive. Are you ready?"

I watch as he starts the engine with a roar, adjusts the rearview mirror to check his hair, flips on the radio to his favorite rock station, flips it off, checks the mirror/hair again, and finally, after what seems like an eternity, puts the car in reverse. Slowly and with much caution, he backs down our long, narrow driveway, which is no easy feat. I am impressed and begin to relax.

Entering the street, he snaps the car into forward and steps on the gas.

"Watch the mailbox! WATCH the mailbox! WATCH THE MAILBOX!" I scream as my foot slams on an imaginary brake.

We miss it by a centimeter.

"See," he says, "no problem."

I rub the cramp in my braking foot as my inexperienced driver pulls out onto a main road with giddy delight.

"Wow, this is fun!" he says, a smile beaming across his face.

Enjoying the new power of his moveable beast, he starts to pick up speed. I tense. Suddenly, all mailboxes, light posts, and assorted garbage cans seem really close to the road. Really close!

"Watch your speed," I say calmly. "Slow down on this curve. Slow down ON THIS CURVE!"

My right foot floors the fake brake as we whip around the bend.

"I'm not going that fast," he argues.

I let out a deep breath. "Just turn right at the next road."

Flipping on his signal, he makes a wide turn directly into the opposite lane. Luckily for our insurance rates, there is no on-coming car.

"You've got to stay in your own lane," I snap.

Silence fills the air. He grips the wheel. I grasp for patience.

Heading down a long stretch of country road in a tension-filled car, I struggle to keep quiet and just let him experience the driving.

Looking around at the countryside for the first time, I notice that the fields are awash in a clear golden light. The late afternoon sun hangs low in the rich blue sky. The warm breeze blowing through the open windows caresses our faces and soothes the tension.

After a period of quiet, my son turns to me with an eager face, happiness shining in his eyes. "How am I doing?" he asks proudly.

"Very well," I reply.

"See, Mama," he says, "you just need to give me more time."

"I know," I say. "You're going to make a great driver."

Smiling brightly, he steps on the gas.

I keep silent. He slows at the curve.

Looking over, I regard the innocent profile of my man-child, whose soft cheeks sport the beginnings of light peach fuzz. Radiating an awakening confidence, his face glows with the realization that vast horizons and new beginnings are stretching out before him, just like the wide-open road we are on.

For a fleeting instant, I feel the magic.

I am no longer the weary forty-six-year-old mother of three with a sometimes overwhelming assortment of responsibilities, but once again the carefree young girl in the driver's seat.

And through this blurry mist of time, a beam of knowledge shines out to me. Thirty years ago, as gravel dust floated down upon us in a stalled car, had my father's own memory of a youth gone by come sparkling back to him?

Gingerly tucking my brake foot under the seat, I notice the sky has turned a rosy hue. I turn and look out the back window.

"Is there a car behind us?" my son asks nervously.

"No, but there's a spectacular sunset," I say. "The sky is filled with beautiful colors. Keep your eyes on the road and I'll describe it to you."

"Hey, I can actually see it in my rearview mirror," he says. "Cool."

Through the open windows, the cool breeze blows in the sweet scent of country at dusk. It refreshes and invigorates us. I take a deep breath. My son checks his hair. Cruising on down the road, we both admire the fields glowing in the twilight.

Waiting Up

A spotlight isn't necessary. The youthful faces of these teenage singers and musicians already radiate light and joy. Eyes sparkling and smiles beaming, the young performers join hands for one last time as they take their final bow. After a year of seemingly endless rehearsals and multiple concerts, these kids have thrown their all into this final production.

Now it's party time.

10:45 P.M.: My seventeen-year-old son, looking grown up in his stage tuxedo, threads his way through the congratulatory crowd to hand us his trombone. His girlfriend, in her shimmering, sequined show dress, joins him, and the two wave a fast goodbye and set off to find their friends.

"What time will you be home?" I call after him.

"I won't be late," he yells back. "I'm tired."

Before we can set an exact time, the vision of sparkling sequins and handsome tux dissolve into the crowd.

Cursed with a tendency to worry, I am not a mother who just lets her kids come home whenever. I need a reasonable time for them to be home, for their own safety as well as for my peace of mind. Until all three sons close their bedroom doors for the night, I rest uneasily.

11:00 P.M.: Trying not to set the worry wheels in motion, I reassure myself that this kid is a responsible senior, past the age of curfew, and at a well-chaperoned party. With college starting next year, it's time I give him more leeway.

1:30 A.M.: I awaken somewhat alarmed. I have not heard my son come home. Exhausted from the week's frenzied pace, perhaps I just didn't hear him. I decide to check. Struggling out from the warm comfort of my bed, I walk down the hall to his room.

No one there.

It's just as he left it. Unmade bed, jeans, underwear, socks, music, hangers, books, and schoolwork strewn everywhere. The usual.

1:45 A.M.: Back in bed and wide awake, I watch shadows of occasional car lights dance upon the bedroom wall. Are those lights slowing? Did they turn at our corner? Surely, I will hear the sound of his key at any minute.

2:00 A.M.: Why isn't he home? He said he wouldn't be late. I call 2:00 a.m. late. The sound of a speeding car sets my heart on edge. Please God, don't let my son be in its path. It is the first of many prayers.

2:15 A.M.: My tossing and turning wakes my husband.

"What's wrong?" he asks sleepily.

"He's not home," I whisper. "Do you think I should call the party?"

"Sure," he mumbles drowsily as he snuggles beneath the covers.

My feet hit cold floor as I head downstairs.

In the bright kitchen light, I search for the number in the phone book. Just as fast as my fingers start to dial, I hang up.

This will seriously embarrass my kid. How many other mothers, especially of sons, are calling to check on their teenagers' whereabouts? Will I sound hysterical? Will I convey a lack of trust?

In my foggy, late-night thinking, I remember the car phone. I dial. No answer. He must still be at the party. Fear, worry, and anger alternate as my sparring partners. I pace.

2:30 A.M.: Time to call. I take a deep breath and dial.

"Hi!" a wide-awake teenage voice answers as rock music thumps in the background.

"Hi!" I reply, as if this is a typical 2:30 a.m. chat. I ask if my son is there.

"Nope," the chipper teenager responds. "He left an hour ago." My stomach churns. My imagination swings into high gear. Where is he? In a ditch? Hijacked? At his girlfriend's house? Should I call and wake up her parents? Now that would earn me the Mother of the Year Award.

2:45 A.M.: Fifteen more minutes. That's it and I call. Forget embarrassment. The heck with humiliation. If he's not there, I'll throw a coat over my nightgown and go find him myself. Pent up with nervous energy, I do the thing I hate most. I clean.

Wash the dishes. Empty the dishwasher. Stow the clutter. Try the car phone. No answer.

Straighten pillows. Pick up newspapers. Throw out magazines. Try the car phone. No answer.

Recycle pop cans. Sweep up crumbs. Put away Nintendo. Try the car phone. No answer.

2:55 A.M.: I take a time-out from my cleaning madness. A short story by one of my twelve-year-old son's friends rests on top of his homework. Seeing that it lists my son as a main character, I cannot resist a quick read. Plopping down on the couch, I am thankful for the new distraction.

To my delight, I discover an adolescent tale filled with interesting characters, intriguing action, and a respectable role for my seventh-grader. Just as the plot thickens, the budding author signs off with a suspenseful "to be continued."

Unsure of her direction, the young writer has placed her trust in her friends by bravely asking for their comments. Recognizing and embracing these innocent first efforts, her friends do not betray her.

"Can't wait to find out what happens!" reads one comment.

"Can I have your autograph now?" reads another.

"I'll be there when you pick up your Pulitzer prize!" reads a third.

The gift of simple faith. No doubts. A basic belief in one another. From twelve-year-olds.

This I ponder in the stillness of the night.

3:05 A.M.: Suddenly I hear the scratching sound of a key turning in the lock. The front door squeaks open. My whole body breathes a sigh of relief. Thank you, God.

"Hi!" my seventeen-year-old says cheerfully. "What are you doing up?"

"Cleaning!" I say cheerfully back, as though it's the most natural thing in the world to be doing at three in the morning. All of my anger and angst evaporates at the sight of him, safely returned.

We go over the details of the night. Stage take-down took longer than expected. Got a second wind at the party. Took girlfriend home. Forgot to turn on car phone.

Reaching up to this six-foot-tall young man, I kiss his whiskered cheek good night and slowly climb the stairs to bed. As I crawl once again between the warm sheets, my husband's sleepy voice greets me. "He made it?"

"Yes," I answer. "He did." Pulling the covers up snugly, I listen as my maturing son turns off the lights and gently closes the door to his room.

3:20 A.M.: For a few short hours, I sleep a peaceful sleep.

Road Shows Remembered

My trick-or-treating days are over. No more night walks through the crunch of fallen leaves. No more blinking, swirling flashlights gleaming on the way to the next neighbor's house. No more scrambling to create an imaginative costume at the last minute. Worst of all, no more candy to collect.

My kids, who have been my ticket to this performance, have simply gotten too old for the show. For a mother who loves Halloween night almost as much as her children do, it is just another checkmark on the long list of childhood activities they are quickly outgrowing. With my youngest son entering high school, I think I've pushed this tradition to the limit. It's time to hang up the candy sack.

For years, the splendor of a rose-washed harvest moon rising up over golden cornfields signaled that this autumn pageant was about to begin. Off we'd hurry to the local pumpkin patch, meticulously selecting our bright orange pumpkins from a field bathed in the silky amber of an October dusk.

As organizer of the pumpkin props, my husband supervised the boys while they zealously scooped stringy seeds out of the gourds. Working with the intensity of professional artists, the guys placed their glowing masterpieces on the fireplace hearth for all to admire. The pumpkins' smoky fragrance immersed the house with warmth and excitement.

I assumed the role of costume designer and contrived a variety of inspirational creations that ranged from the toddler-sized furry bear suit (it looked more like a carpet with ears) to the coordinated costumes of Batman, Joker, and Robin, and the Three Amigos.

Not surprisingly, early adolescence brought a desire for costuming independence. I gave up my designated role and left the decision-making to the performers themselves. Like actors preparing for their parts, they rummaged through the basement and closets, coming up with a variety of old hats, jackets, and amazing accessories. An inspired persona always emerged on opening night.

So each October 31, as a red sun sank dramatically behind a backdrop of silhouetted trees, the boys and I headed out into the dusky evening theater. With glowing porch pumpkins as our stage lights, my jubilant children skipped down the driveway in a procession of magnificently creative attire, candy sacks, and flashlights.

Their father stayed behind in the role of treats dispenser. With a good football game on, a quiet house, and a big bowl of candy all to himself, he was a happy man.

Across the yard, the boys ran to pick up their neighborhood friend who, as an only child, delighted in assuming the role of a fourth brother with my sons. (I tried to ignore the fact that his mother, an art teacher, created fabulously perfect costumes.)

Because we live on the outskirts of town, with houses spread far apart and few streetlights, his mom and I always accompanied the boys. In truth, Halloween provided us with the perfect excuse to walk under the stars, smell the damp scent of newly fallen leaves, and, most importantly, enjoy this escapade with our sons.

When the guys were little, they were content to walk by our sides and hold our hands. As they got bigger, they dashed ahead to the next neighbor's house until we called for them to wait. Before long, it wasn't cool to have moms with bright flashlights in sight. As the boys dashed from house to house, we hung back, following behind them in the darkness.

Every now and then, they would stop, unsure of where we were.

"Mom?" one would call out in the darkness.

"Right here," we'd answer, blinking our flashlights on and off like fireflies.

Relieved, they'd run off through the next yard. We could hear their laughter and squeals of joy when they received an exceptionally good treat. Then suddenly all would be still.

"Mom?" they'd call again.

"Here we are," we'd shout, flashing our lights from the side of the road, not as far away as they thought.

And so it would go.

Each year brought a thrilling and poignant performance. There were nights that the stars shone in the heavens like brightly lit lanterns to guide our way. We pointed out the constellations as we walked down a road skirted by open fields.

There were nights when a mist or drizzle made the leaves more pungent, and the woods and fields refreshed us with their fragrance.

There were nights when the moon was full, and all was lit with grandeur and beauty.

And there were freezing cold nights when snowflakes made a surprise appearance. Falling softly from a cloud-coated sky, they dusted us in sparkling splendor as we marched along.

Best of all, there were nights filled with great camaraderie, laughter, good visits, the drama of disguise, and the mystery of a walk in the dark. Nights of enchantment and joy.

Then one year, my oldest son, at about thirteen, realized that perhaps it was time for him to exit this show. A few seasons later, our middle son and our neighbor's son bowed out. My youngest and I continued this long-running act with a couple of his buddies as extra cast members, but we have finally crossed the threshold of an activity outgrown.

So we won't be going out this year. It's time to close the curtain on a magical night. The scenery was magnificent, the costumes delightful, and the characters the finest with whom I could ever hope to share a stage.

This year, I'll be waiting in the wings. I'll pull a chair up to the window with a glowing pumpkin by my side and wait for my little neighborhood friends to come by. When they do, I'll compliment them on their wonderfully inspired attire, give them an extra treat or two, and watch with envy as they skip down my driveway to the glimmer of a waiting flashlight and fade into the night.

Then, I think I'll sit back and help myself to a candy bar or two.

Back to School Blues

The house is too quiet. The phone has stopped ringing. The TV sits silent. No maddening video game music comes from the porch. Outside, the basketball hoop stands like a lonely sentry on an empty driveway. The laughter and shouting that rebounded there this summer are now just echoes.

Three basketballs, a dented Whiffle ball and bat, a pile of muddy golf balls and one rusty club, and two worn footballs are scattered like confetti across the yard where they were all abandoned for the next game of choice. In a brief moment, the action has all stopped.

Today is the first day of school.

Although many parents look forward to this day after a long summer of kids underfoot, I find it somewhat unsettling. Perhaps it's because my three boys are teenagers, only a few ball bounces away from their own independent lives. I know that the quiet I hear today will be a permanent sound in the not-too-distant future.

To be honest, there's a lot about the summer teen scene I won't miss. At the top of the list are the aforementioned messes. They appear with amazing regularity, no matter how often I direct the boys to pick up. Remnants of orange Kool-Aid sprinkled on the counter, pop cans deserted exactly where the last sip occurred, a minefield of shoes scattered at every entrance, newspapers left throughout the house, chip bags tucked into a variety of obscure places—under the bed or in the bathroom cupboard.

Add to this mess the scramble of their summer activities—band camps, team practices, summer jobs, sport camps, vacations with family, and trips with friends—and our calendar looked like a spiderweb gone haywire.

Throw in staggered curfews for a fourteen-, a sixteen-, and a nineteen-year-old, and my husband and I were up all hours of the night, like summer camp counselors on the midnight shift.

So what will I miss about the boys' summer time at home? A lot. I'll miss the energetic sound of a basketball thumping on the driveway. The chance encounter of a good one-on-one visit in the kitchen. The kids' lively banter as they play pool on the porch.

I'll miss glimpsing the sweet innocence of young love as my oldest and his girlfriend cuddle on the couch watching videos. I'll miss my younger sons' sleepovers with their buddies, the late-night smells of pizza and popcorn, the low rhythms of their rock music, the voices of happy boys drifting through the house.

Most of all, I'll miss the daily opportunities to witness my sons' gentle metamorphoses into young men. Under the soft summer skies, I observed their joy at trying new things, their adolescent disappointments and courageous comebacks, their delight in accomplishing their goals.

Sometimes, in quiet moments, each son spoke of a summer experience and cultivated it into deeper expressions of thoughts and feelings. As a gardener tending the most precious of blooms, I gathered the essence of their youthful spirits and hugged them close to my heart.

But every growing season must come to an end. One bright, sunny morning, the school bell beckoned, and out the door, one by one, they went.

With the back end of his used pickup piled high with boxes, a worn stuffed chair, and his computer, my oldest son pulled confidently out of the driveway and headed off to his second year of college. As he turned the corner, the early morning light caught the gleam of his brass trombone perched on a laundry basket, and in a sparkle, he was gone.

A few minutes later, my second son eagerly backed the car out of the garage to begin his junior year of high school. My youngest son, a freshman, jubilant at finally not having to ride the bus, climbed in next to him. Their faces beamed with delight in mutual anticipation of this new independence. With a happy honk and blasting radio, out the driveway they went.

As I re-enter the house, the quiet grips me. All is still. Even the dog senses that something has changed. He posts himself by the front window and begins his vigil of watching and waiting for the boys' return.

At a momentary loss as to what to do, I grab a sponge and slowly scrub the last of the Kool-Aid stains from the kitchen counter. This simple chore gives me a moment to regroup and reflect. With my youngest off to high school, I know that in four short years, this phase of my life will be over.

Much like the first days of kindergarten, these back-to-school days bring an exciting sense of new beginnings for both parents and children, and also the recognition that this time of togetherness is fleeting.

So, on this first day of school, although a myriad of responsibilities await me, I think I'll bounce this stillness away and go shoot a few baskets. The sounds of a thumping ball will ease my lonely heart.

The Sound of Peace

They stand straight and tall. Age has not withered their pride. A small ensemble of World War II veterans in tightly buttoned uniforms form a line for the start of the ceremony. Gray hair sticks out from under their caps; deep lines crease their faces. At the sound of a sharp command, the color guard moves forward, wavering slightly under the weight of their flags. Their shuffling feet struggle to keep in step.

A second sharp command brings them to a standstill. Ready. Aim. With great effort, those with rifles cock their weapons and pull the triggers. Fire! The explosions throw their frail bodies slightly off balance. Again. Point. Aim. Fire! The gun blasts reverberate through the air, shocking the small crowd into hushed stillness.

Veterans Day in our town is always observed in a dignified and respectful manner. The ceremony rotates between the east- and west-side cemeteries; if the weather is inclement, it is held at the local VFW hangar. The service is short, to the point, and always moving.

The high school brass ensemble often leads off with the low notes of an old military hymn. An invocation, introductions, thank-yous, a short address, the Pledge of Allegiance, and "The Star-Spangled Banner" follow. The service ends with a rifle salute to fallen comrades, the placing of wreaths, and the playing of taps by one of the high school trumpeters.

With the exception of the high school brass ensemble, the group is mostly elderly. Gray heads, walkers, and canes dot the crowd. Conversations center on knee-replacement surgeries and other health-related issues. Most of those in attendance seem to know each other. They've been here before.

I think about the aging faces I see in the color guard. It is not hard to envision them in their fading uniforms as handsome young men, strong and vibrant. The Vietnam vet who is now our local sheriff gives the main address. He speaks passionately about MIAs and POWs. He sounds and looks tough, yet tears unabashedly slide down his face. I wonder about his memories. Is he close to someone who is not accounted for?

I sit in my folding chair at the back of the room as an observer. I am not part of the camaraderie that holds most of these people together. And for that I am extremely grateful. I do not want war memories. I am here because one of my sons has volunteered to play with the high school brass ensemble.

I watch my sixteen-year-old son as he holds his trumpet, ready to play taps. He is handsome and strong. Full of enthusiasm and vitality. I think of other mothers before me who must have thought the same about their sons as they sent them off to war.

The price of peace. Here in this little ceremony is a snippet of what it takes.

I am glad that my son and his brother before him have volunteered to play in the brass ensemble at this Veterans Day ceremony. Their grandfathers, now deceased, served overseas in the navy and army during World War II. They would be proud.

I think of their grandmother's cousin who was an eight-year POW in the Vietnam War and the strength and courage it must have taken him to survive. I think of my best friend from kindergarten whose husband has served as a captain in the navy, making the military his lifetime career. I think of a couple of my oldest son's buddies, fresh-faced twenty-year-olds heading off for a stint in the marines or air force, full of enthusiasm and a zest for life. All give faces to our freedom.

With the speeches now over, it is time for taps. Fingering the keys of his trumpet, my son appears slightly nervous. He is a sensitive kid, and I know he feels the weight of what this melody means to so many who sit in the audience. Lifting the silver horn to his lips, he takes a deep breath and plays the song strong and sweet and clear. A fellow high school trumpeter softly echoes the notes from a secluded distance. The air seems filled with poignant memories.

I have heard my son play taps many times before, in much less solemn but equally compelling circumstances. He often brings his trumpet up to the Northwoods to the little log cabin built by his great-grandparents. In anticipation of school band tryouts, he will often practice there.

Sometimes, as the summer sun sets brilliantly over the silver waters of the lake, he is inspired to play taps. He stands on a wooded hill, silhouetted against the rosy gold of the sky. In this world where eagles fly and loons call, the peace at the end of the day, like the pine scent in the air, is almost tangible. The trumpet's clear notes float across the water like waves gently lapping against the shore. A soothing stillness seems to permeate the forest and lake. Even the birds are hushed.

Day is done.

The red glow of the sunset fills the sky.

Gone the sun.

A sprinkling of sparkling stars begins to appear.

From the lake, from the hills, from the sky.

Dusk softly falls.

All is well, safely rest.

Peacefulness permeates our souls.

God is nigh.

The last clear notes of the trumpet fade across the lake and echo into the forest.

The sound of peace.

For the vets who served us and the children who follow, may it always be so.

Listen To What I Hear

As always, the phone call came at the last minute.

"So when are we taking the boys Christmas caroling?" asked my neighbor Mary, cheerful beyond measure with only five days left before Christmas.

Christmas caroling? Was she crazy? The December 25 deadline for shopping, wrapping, baking, and cleaning loomed like an apparition over Scrooge's head.

Who had time to sing?

Yet I knew that passing up the opportunity to take my three young sons and Mary's little guy out into the crisp night air to sing carols for our neighbors would haunt me like the Ghost of Christmas Past.

"How does the twenty-third look?" I asked, mustering as much enthusiasm as I could.

"Perfect!" said Mary, who doubles as a highly organized art teacher. "I'll send out flyers for our neighbors to leave their porch lights on if they'd like us to stop. You bring the hot chocolate."

With that she hung up. There was no backing out now. The event was rolling along like the final verses of the "Hallelujah Chorus."

"When are we going Christmas caroling?" asked an eager son hovering nearby.

"The day after tomorrow," I answered.

"I get the sleigh bells this year!" all three yelled together.

Two days later, the mystery of a winter night beckoned, dark and frosty. The three boys and I stuffed ourselves into as much warm clothing as allowed us to move, filled the thermos with hot chocolate, grabbed a bag of cups and marshmallows, and snatched the sleigh bells from the mantel.

Just about the time we started to sweat, Mary called to say they were on their way.

"Meet you at the end of the driveway," she said.

"Let's go!" the boys yelled, dashing out the door into the welcome blast of cold night air.

Down the hill and across the street came Mary and Brad. As we gathered in the road, the boys let out whoops of joy at the sight that greeted us.

"Wow! Look at that!" Brad said.

Mary's flyer had done the trick. A beacon of porch lights, like a string of constellations, twinkled around our horseshoe-shaped lane, directing us to a waiting audience.

"We better do a warm-up before we go," Mary suggested.

Like a rowdy Midwestern version of an English boys' choir, our four guys launched into a rousing rendition of "Jingle Bells," our opener, ringing their bells with enough gusto to spook even Marley's ghost. As they hit the last note, they were off and running to the nearest house to see who could push the doorbell first. Mary and I lagged behind, struggling to keep up with their energy.

As soon as a neighbor swung open the storm door, the boys broke into song. One by one, more friendly faces began to pop up behind the first one until we had a small ensemble bobbing in tune with our beat. Ending our short medley with "We Wish You a Merry Christmas," the boys were often rewarded with candy canes or Christmas cookies.

Of course, Mary and I had to have some too.

Then it was on to the next welcoming porch light as more shivering neighbors shouted to family members, "Come quickly, it's the Christmas carolers!"

After five or six houses, our throats were ready for a short intermission. Sipping the soothing hot cocoa, we looked skyward through the sculpted arms of a huge old oak tree, studied the stars, and embraced the sudden stillness of the night.

In that simple moment, I found the peace of Christmas.

But soon the rustle of jingling bells indicated it was time to move on. One of our favorite stops was at Bill and Paula's. Although Bill's speech was impaired from a stroke, he opened the door like a king welcoming his favorite minstrels to his court. Paula appeared right behind him with an array of cookies made just for us.

The boys' repertoire for Bill differed slightly from the rest. They knew his favorite song was "Silent Night," and they sang it with all the awkward tenderness that their innocent young voices could muster.

A moment of magic hung in the air, like a snowflake drifting through a moonlit night, as the boys ended their song. With misted eyes, Bill broke into enthusiastic applause and with great effort called each boy by name.

"J-John, B-Bob, T-Tom, and B-Brad, that was wonderful!" he joyfully proclaimed.

The boys beamed with the awareness that they had given a gift.

As our guys grew older, musical instruments began to replace the bells. Two trombones, a trumpet, and a drummer often made up our caroling band, with Mary and me as backup singers.

Some years we sang in soft snowfall, and some years the nights were so cold the boys' instruments stuck to their lips. Sometimes visiting grandmothers trudged along beside us, and occasionally the voices of new children who had moved into the neighborhood joined the swell. Once we even sang "Away in a Manager" to a neighbor's stabled horse.

Always there were porch lights beckoning and sweet songs answering.

Sometime during the boys' teenage years, however, Mary's caroling phone call stopped coming. Band concerts, dates, and sports took over the boys' busy schedules, and we all moved on to other Christmas activities.

Like the imperceptible beat of angel wings, time flew by. Our boys became young men, Bill passed on, and after twenty-six years as my neighbor, Mary moved away.

Yet even now, when the hectic holidays threaten to turn me into a humbug, I'll step out into the night and look up through the gnarled arms of an old oak to the sparkling stars. The cold quiet warms my soul. And if I listen closely, I can hear the peace of Christmas in the whisper of young boys' voices serenading back to me, "All is calm, all is bright . . ."

The echo, forever, will be a hymn in my heart.

Comes an Echo on the Breeze

The kid is leaving. It's been only three days since his college graduation ceremony, yet my firstborn is ready to strike out on his own. In the early morning light, as the sweet songs of waking birds fill the air, he stuffs the flashlight I insist he take with him into an already jam-packed car. Then, with a happy honk and a hearty wave, he pulls out of our driveway and heads west to a new life.

I wave cheerfully and shout "Happy trails!" as he rounds the corner, goes over the hill, and drives out of sight. Then I turn, walk into my husband's arms, and sob my heart out.

Twenty-two years. Born, raised, and out the door. Our job as parents of our firstborn is essentially done. As I stand in the driveway in my old green bathrobe, letting the warm morning sunshine soothe my hurting heart, I realize I am not prepared for this moment of separation and all that it means. The fact that he is moving twenty-six hundred miles away only accentuates the point. He is the first to leave the nest, and it is not easy.

I have never been good at parent-child separations. I have too much of the mother bear instinct. Worries and fears about the unknown overwhelm me when my cubs are out of sight. Fortunately, my children do not feel the same. They bound out the door to new experiences with joy, anticipation, and a sense of adventure.

The day my oldest headed off to kindergarten was no exception. Despite a gentle rain, he insisted on standing outside, not wanting to miss a moment of his new journey. He stood on the corner in a little yellow slicker, eagerly awaiting the school bus, while I paced nervously back and forth. When the bus finally rumbled over the hill and stopped for him, he looked back at me, gave a merry wave, and hopped aboard.

He's never looked back.

When he was twelve, we went through our first extended overnight separation when we drove him to a weeklong music camp. Although I knew it would be a wonderful experience for him, I sat in the passenger seat on the drive down, knitting needles flying, fretting about leaving him on such a big campus. What if he got sick? Could he get lost? Would he make friends?

Yet for him, those challenges meant learning to take care of himself, navigating an unfamiliar environment, and meeting a diverse mix of kids. He had a blast.

When he was sixteen, he jumped at the opportunity to travel to Italy with his Latin teacher and class. This was our first long-distance separation, and I was a total wreck. How could I let him fly over the Atlantic Ocean without me? Would he be able to communicate? Would he be safe exploring on his own?

Yet for him, those challenges meant the thrilling adventure of flying (without me) over a vast ocean to a foreign land, learning to communicate with people not like him, and sharing insights with his peers on the beauty of Italy's historic art and architecture. It was a wonderful education.

The day we took him off to college, I held my breath. This was real separation. On his own. Total freedom. Choices to be made. Responsibilities to be met. I knew that, as his mother, I was fading out of the picture. He was testing his wings, and I had to step back.

Four fast years later, we found ourselves at his commencement, listening to the regal rhythm of "Pomp and Circumstance" and wondering where all the time had gone.

Despite his mother's worrying and fretting over the years, he is confident and strong, just as I want him to be. I am grateful that he has the self-assurance to embark on new adventures. I wouldn't want it any other way. And in my heart, I understand it is what he needs.

As the ceremony drew to a close, the university choir serenaded the rows of seated family members with our state song, "Illinois." A deep voice sang the lovely lyrics against a background of harmony:

> By thy rivers gently flowing, Illinois, Illinois,
> O'er the prairies verdant growing, Illinois, Illinois,
> Comes an echo on the breeze,
> Rustling through the leafy trees,
> And its mellow tones are these, Illinois.

My prayer for my son, as he crosses new prairies and fords distant rivers, is to always listen for the "echo on the breeze." It is the sound of our love for him always.

At our fourth-generation log cabin on a lake deep in the Northwoods, our family has always rung an old metal bell when someone leaves at the end of a stay. We stand outside and wave and shout with gusto, ringing the bell loudly until the friend or family member drives out of sight. For the one driving away, it is a happy and joyous sound.

And so on this beautiful early morning, as you drive around the corner and over the hill, although I do not have the bell with me, know that it is ringing in my heart loud and clear. Happy trails, my son. Happy trails.

Changing Course

It's hard to see down the road. The pouring rain and hot summer mist create a veil across the fields of corn as I drive my youngest child off to his two-day college orientation.

It's been a week since his high school graduation, and we have hit a lull. The excitement and anticipation of the ceremony are over. Now the future hovers with uncertainty. In the fall, he will leave all that he has loved and known for a new life, and I will return to an empty nest.

With jangled nerves, we pull in to campus and check in to his overnight dorm. As he heads upstairs to his room, I pace nervously around and somehow enter the men's bathroom. (I don't know who looked more surprised, the two young men or me.) Meanwhile, he has mistakenly walked into the wrong room and met the wrong roommate. We are off to a shaky start.

The morning improves, however, when my son makes small talk with the kid behind him in line and coincidentally discovers it's his roommate for the fall. Big sigh of relief. He has a friend.

Next, I check into my dorm across campus. I'm not happy about having to share a room with a stranger after our kids dump us off at nine o'clock for their evening of activities. I'll just want to read my book and go to sleep, not make small talk.

As I unlock my dorm door, my roommate happens to arrive at the same time. Her friendly smile and easy conversation put me at ease. We both head out to our separate activities a little less anxious.

The first orientation session focuses on planning the students' fall schedules. Until this point, my son has wanted to major in history education. As we listen to the information, he casually turns to me and whispers that he wants to switch his major to acting.

Acting?

I remain calm.

Although he has nonchalantly mentioned this once or twice in the last few weeks, the kid is now seriously testing the waters. We both know the odds of "success" are slim, which means this $18,000 annual tuition bill might lead to a career as headwaiter.

But who am I to say, "No. You have to be a history teacher"?

"Acting?" he asks with hopeful eyes as he gets up to leave with his academic advising group.

"Go for it, kid," I say as he heads out the door.

Waiting for our parents' session to begin, I think back to the start of my own college days. I can clearly remember what I wore my first day on campus: a navy blue shirtwaist dress with a red apple pin anchored to its Peter Pan collar and red flats to match.

However, as the year was 1967, I soon traded the dresses and pins for bell-bottoms and beads. The anti-establishment attitude, feminist movement, and Vietnam protests were just heating up.

Being at a university during this poignant historic period led me through all sorts of twists and turns, achievements, disappointments, and new experiences. Yet, looking back, I am grateful for the opportunity to grow, the exposure to vastly different viewpoints, and the challenge to really think on my own.

I cannot say, as many do, that it was the happiest time of my life, but I can say that I learned a lot about myself and the world. In that sense, my college education was a huge success. I can only hope for the same for my son, no matter what choices he makes or opportunities he pursues.

Later that night when my roommate, Darlene, and I are back in our room, we discover we are both 1967 high school grads. We compare notes and laugh about the similarities of our college days. Soon we are discussing our dreams for our children about to embark on theirs.

When I mention that my son wants to major in acting, Darlene is encouraging. When she discusses her daughter's desire to balance soccer, a business honors program, and dance team, I respond in kind.

We talk late into the night, finally drifting off to sleep, no longer strangers but friends and mothers with similar hopes for our children. Our books lie unread beside our beds. We would have made good college roommates.

The sky is sunny and clear as my son and I leave campus the next day. The kid drives. He is now officially an acting major. We enthusiastically fill each other in on information we gathered at our different sessions.

Winding our way back home through the cornfield-lined highways, we listen to each other's music. He plays for me two versions of Bob Dylan's "Knockin' on Heaven's Door" by Eric Clapton and Guns N' Roses. I play for him Carole King and James Taylor. He sings to his tunes. I sing to mine. Sometimes we sing together.

The song I hope he listens to most, this dear child of mine, is the melody of his heart. As he flies away and leaves my nest empty, it matters not if he becomes an actor on the big screen, a history teacher in a small town, or headwaiter in a fancy restaurant. I'll be there.

Just listen for my applause.

Forever Friends

You will remember a curve of your wagon track in the grass of the plain, like the features of a friend.

—Isak Dinesen

Still Afloat at Fifty

"Fit and fabulous at fifty!" This was our motto. Around age forty-eight, my two best friends from childhood and I (who together dealt with bikes, bras, and boyfriends, in no particular order) decided over a long leisurely lunch that we needed some motivation to meet the half-century mark.

"We'll be fit! We'll be fabulous! We'll be fifty!" we shouted to the annoyance of neighboring lunchers who wondered if our hearing had gone bad.

"Let's do it!" we yelled. (We didn't spend years cheerleading for nothing.)

Alas, two years later, here we are. Each, in our own time, labeled with the big fifty vintage upon our bottled necks. Fit? It's more than iffy. Fabulous? It's in the eye of the beholder. So, forget the fit and fabulous. Much like a kaleidoscope that fractures images into startling surprises, the real fifty produces unexpected results.

First off, fifty is freeing. For Martha (my best friend from kindergarten) and me, riding our bikes together through leafy, sunlit streets from one house to another was a favorite activity. The best moments came when we headed down a little hill, the wind whipping our hair and cooling our faces on a hot summer day. At fifty, I know it's metaphorically time to capture that feeling again. The trail has a finish line. It's a now-or-never moment to jettison old baggage and hang-ups, let go of the brakes, and ride for the joy of it.

Fifty is also about forgiving. The snubs, the cross words, the unintended hurts seem less significant and easier to forget. At fifty, the brilliance of old friendships or the beauty of a sibling's enduring love can shine through the muddiness that clouds even the best of relationships. At fifty, one becomes more acutely aware of the rare gifts these friends and family members are in our lives. These treasured connections take on the light and luster of high-quality gems. Yes, there are still flaws, but that is what makes the relationships all the more precious.

And finally, fifty is about the physical. It's about coming to terms with one's body and accepting what one has or doesn't have. Yes, it would be nice to look like the model in the health club ad, but at fifty that dream has definitely gone up in smoke.

Isn't it wonderful that Renoir painted arms like mine on his lovely lady in *The Laundress*? These arms might be flabby, but they can still sail a boat solo across the rough and windy waters of a Northwoods lake.

These legs might no longer earn the Best Legs Award I received in high school, but they can still get me up onto a slalom water ski on the first pull. What more could I want? Fifty brings a sense of physical peace.

I spent my fiftieth birthday with my family and a few dear friends on the beloved lake of our family's 1929 log cabin where I celebrated my first birthday, as well as at least forty others. It was a simple, yet joyous day. Fifty *is* fit and fabulous. To have good health, friends, and to be loved certainly makes it so.

Shortly after my birthday, with my family scattered to their various responsibilities, my almost eighty-year-old mother and I shared a few last days of summer on the lake together. Sitting on our weathered dock in the August sun, we watched the waves sail rhythmically down the lake and listened to a soft wind rustle the branches of the white pines that my grandmother planted along the shore over seventy years ago.

Stepping with comic ungracefulness into the water to cool off, we discussed the milestones in age that we had each reached. As we waded across the sandy bottom, gingerly sprinkling ourselves with the cold water, we acknowledged that inwardly we both felt at least twenty years younger.

"I have to admit though," I confided to my mother. "At fifty, it's hard knowing that I've definitely left my youth behind. I could fool myself for a bit in my forties, but at fifty, it's definitely gone."

Without missing a beat, my mother looked me squarely in the eye. "Just look at it from my point of view," she said. "Oh, to be fifty again!"

"Let's swim," I said.

With that, we waded farther out, took a deep breath, and plunged into the cold water, diving deep to follow the old family tradition of "clearing the cobwebs from our heads."

"Refreshing!" my mother said as she popped to the surface.

"Exhilarating!" I answered with a splash.

After several laps out and back, we floated on our backs and gazed up at emerald pines framed against a deep blue sky. An eagle swirled high overhead, do-si-doing with the wispy clouds that danced across the heavens.

Perhaps from her lofty perch, the eagle gazed down upon a "middle-aged" daughter and her "elderly" mother bobbing contentedly side by side on the waves, happy for the warmth of a late summer sun upon their faces.

I like to think she tipped her wings in fellowship.

Synchronized Heartbeats

It was the hat that got my attention. Two feet of white faux fur strapped jauntily on his head, a stunning accoutrement to his white drum major's uniform with gold buttons that glinted in the stadium lights.

The year was 1963. As a high school freshman, I had been asked by a sophomore to homecoming. Since neither of us could drive, my date snared a junior who could. Warm autumn breezes filled the night as my homecoming date steered me toward the band section of the bleachers to introduce me to the driver of our car. In the midst of cheering football fans, a handsome drum major stood up and doffed his monstrous chapeau to greet me.

With all due respect to the hat, it was his warm, smiling green eyes that sparked my heart. Even though he was seventeen and I was only fourteen, I knew instantly that something magical had happened.

And I was right. Within a year, we became high school sweethearts, dated steadily for five years, and married when I was twenty. Thirty years later, we're still here, happy together.

"How did you know he was the right one at such a young age?" friends will often ask.

"Young and dumb," is my glib reply.

"Didn't you date anyone else?" is the next shocked question.

Being older, he had several girlfriends before me, and I dated someone else for three months during my senior year. But mostly, it was just the two of us.

During our five-year dating period, we held hands a lot, called each other Buddy, and, when we weren't kissing, laughed often at each other's attempts at humor. Thirty years later, it's still pretty much the same, only now we hold hands to help each other up, call each other Mom and Dad, sneak in the kissing, and laugh because we can't hear what the other said.

With marital longevity under our belts and the last of our three sons leaving home for college, we're suddenly aware that we actually still like each other. I've heard many happy couples attribute their marital success to hard work, but I must confess the opposite. It has never been work. It's only been easy.

It's easy to love a man who has washed the dinner dishes all of our married life, serenaded me on the piano by candlelight when the electricity went out the night before our first child was born, and built fires at 2:00 a.m. on cold winter nights to keep me warm as I nursed a newborn.

It's easy to love a man who planted a whole row of blooming daffodils at the edge of our woods one Mother's Day, played ball for hours in our yard with our sons, and canoed with me on my fiftieth birthday out to see the sunrise on the same Northwoods lake where we celebrated my sixteenth birthday together.

On our sixth wedding anniversary, my mother found us unromantically varnishing doors outside in the hot sun and called our marriage "glorious." Henceforth, we have humorously toasted each successive year, despite the challenges of jobs, children, and home, as glorious.

Has it been perfect? Of course not. Do we argue? Sometimes. Do we disagree? Occasionally. Have we hurt each other? Sure.

But like a lovely woodland wildflower that is accidentally stepped on and then springs back up, our love is resilient. We know that what we have is too precious to lose. So we are fast to forgive. Quick to compromise. Eager to laugh.

This preciousness was brought into sharper focus a year ago when my husband went in for a routine stress test and, two hours later, underwent an angioplasty for 70 percent blockage in his heart.

As a lean, lifelong runner with low blood pressure, my husband was shocked at the sudden turn of events. Called out of work, I raced to the hospital. Things moved too quickly for us to notify our children. With false bravery, we tried to give strength and encouragement to the other.

"Here's where you have to stop," the nurse told me.

To bend down and kiss your high school sweetheart, father of your children, and best friend goodbye under such unnerving circumstances is no easy task. In the moment before the nurse briskly rolled him away, our "I love yous" and goodbye kisses suddenly took on a whole new depth.

By the grace of God and an excellent surgeon, all went well. The experience only made our love stronger and re-emphasized that every day together is a gift.

On a recent getaway to our Northwoods cabin, we celebrated the one-year anniversary of his healthy recovery with a champagne toast. As we sat by the fire, I pondered the success of our marriage.

"Why do you think we've been happy?" I asked. "Do you think we've just been lucky?"

"Nope," he answered without missing a beat. "It's just plain love."

After all these glorious years, even without the hat, he's still sparking my heart.

No Place to Run

Only five could make it. It was 1966, the spring of our junior year, and cheerleading tryouts for our local high school loomed like a cliffhanger on a popular soap opera.

In a school of over fifteen hundred students, cheerleading was the only team open to girls. There were no competitive sports for girls—no tennis, no golf, no track, no cross-country, no volleyball, no softball, and certainly no basketball. The reasoning, of course, was that we might sweat! We might get emotional! And certainly we couldn't handle the competition!

Sure, there was the GAA (Girls Athletic Association), but that mostly involved standing around after school batting a shuttlecock back and forth in unorganized games of badminton.

Naturally, there was gym class, but even during the basketball unit, our play was limited to "girls' rules," which meant you could take only three dribbles before passing the ball, and you couldn't run past half-court.

Now who dreamed that up?

And although one young teacher started a gymnastics club where we could hone our skills on the rings or trampoline, that was about it for exercise.

All that lack of competitive sports for girls meant there was no place to run. No place to jump. No place to catch a ball, learn about team togetherness, share the camaraderie of a locker room, or work with a coach. We girls were definitely designated to the sidelines to sit and watch the boys. And with all those raging hormones, that was not a good thing.

There was only one athletic opportunity for us, and it wasn't even considered a sport. It was cheerleading.

Because there were only five spots on the squad, the competition was tough, to say the least, and so we started practicing months in advance. Gathering in a friend's backyard, we unselfishly helped each other fine-tune our cheers, hone our arm movements, and perfect our back jumps.

These back jumps involved flinging our bodies up into the air and bending them backward to form the curve of a reverse *C*, the goal being to touch your heels to your head. The more you knocked your head, the better you were. In the school fight song, "Roll On," this jump was initiated from a squatting position on the floor. Can there be anything more athletic than that?

On tryout day, the electricity in the gym air rivaled that of an Olympic stadium. Our stomachs were in knots, not to mention the muscles of our backs.

Adding to our nervousness was the fact that we had to try out in front of the entire student council, which numbered well over one hundred, including the dozens of curious students who came to enjoy the spectacle. Shakespeare could not have dreamed up a finer drama.

We headed out two by two, as if onto Noah's Ark, to test our survival.

When at last all the partnered rounds were completed, we competitors were sequestered in the cavernous, dark gray girls' locker room to await our fate. Hot and sweaty from the physical exertion and our nerves, we huddled side by side and silently prayed that one of the names called out would be ours.

After a torturously long wait, the winners were called out one by one to a cheering crowd.

"Lucinda!" boomed through the humid, still air of the locker room. Hugs all around and out she ran to the roar of applause waiting back in the gym.

"Martha!" We kissed her and sent her on her way.

"Patty!" We looked around to see who was left.

"Carolyn!" We held our breath. One spot remained.

"Marnie!" In disbelief, I ran out to join the other four, and for the first time we performed the school fight song together.

And, yes, we cried.

But not for long! Our new team had work to do.

We practiced often. We created new cheers. We added the splits to our routines. We yelled till we were hoarse, jumped till our backs ached, cheered till our arms could hardly move. And through all that grueling work, we did what boys never do while out on the court: we smiled!

Although a few of us were blond, we were not ditzy. We were class officers and members of the band, a cappella choir, student council, National Honor Society, and numerous other organizations. But best of all we were good friends. Even though we were not a clique, spending so much time together drew us closer.

When one of us was having a bad day, the other four listened. When one of us needed encouragement, we offered her a pep talk. And on the rare occasions when we got miffed with one another, we forgave.

But mostly we laughed. Doubled-over, split-your-gut laughter.

Take the Taylorville Basketball Tournament. Because the boys' teams were using both locker rooms and no arrangements had been made for the cheerleaders, we had to use the referees' shower and sidestep a pink jock strap that had been left on the shower floor. Butt naked, we laughed till our sides split at the absurdity of the situation.

Then there was the American Midwest Cheerleading Competition held at the Palmer House in Chicago. Waiting for our turn to compete, we did some amazing detective work and tracked down Jack Benny, who was there for a performance.

Boldly we knocked on his hotel room door.

To our surprise, he answered.

"Hi!" we chirped.

"Oh, girls," he said, rolling his eyes and promptly shutting the door in our faces.

We laughed ourselves silly all the way back down to the competition, one of the first of its kind, which, by the way, we won, beating out dozens of other Chicago-area teams. I don't think it made the papers.

And then there were our mad dashes to the games. Whether we were dining at each other's homes in our pregame tradition, enjoying a meal lovingly prepared by our mothers, or gulping down greasy burgers from the Big Boy restaurant (the irony of the name was not lost on us), we always managed to be running late. With minutes to go, we would race into the gym just as the buzzer sounded and the pep band swung into the school song.

Crazed with laughter at our constant tardiness, we launched into those back jumps from the floor on full stomachs and undigested suppers. I am proud to say, we never threw up.

We cheered in rain and snow, did back jumps from the sharp cinder track of the football field, sweated in heavy wool sweaters, and twirled for our last season in the beautiful American Indian–themed dresses with fringed sleeves that represented our Blackhawk name.

Cheer after cheer, we fired up the crowd and the crowd cheered back. (We were leaders before our time in crowd management and, in today's lingo, created multiparticipatory and interactive events involving several hundred people.)

For one glorious year, we jumped, we ran, we worked out, and yes, we learned about sportsmanship, teamwork, the challenges of sore muscles, and the camaraderie that develops out of late night talks on a game bus home. When the season ended, so did our brief athletic fame. We graduated and went on to college, but managed to keep in touch over the years, no matter how many hundreds of miles separated us or how different our lives became. When sweet, beautiful Patty was tragically killed in a car crash at age thirty, we cherished the precious gift of our friendship all the more.

Nowadays, the four of us are rarely together, but with Lucinda flying in from California for a family visit and the three of us nearby, we will reunite. Lucinda's eighty-one-year-old mother, Kally, still a loyal Blackhawk fan, has organized a basketball kick-off party for thirty of her closest friends. She thinks it will be hysterical if the four of us perform "Roll On" in some cheerleading sweaters she has mysteriously "borrowed" from the high school.

We did this once before at Kally's request, and, let me tell you, there is no dignity left for four fifty-six-year-old women doing the school fight song in sweaters two sizes too small. Back jumps are definitely out, but bust-your-gut laughter is not.

Oh, and guess what? The Illinois High School Association finally recognized cheerleading as a sport.

You go, girls! All together now! Yeaaaaaaa Team!

Shuffle and Deal

It's poker night. The hand is five-card stud. The pot is nickel, dime, quarter. The most the boys can lose is ten bucks.

The "boys" are eight high school buddies from the class of 1965, sitting around a dining room table with pretzel sticks, peanut M&Ms, a pile of chips, and a deck of cards. They've been dealing out this fun for over thirty years.

At this point in time, no one in the group can quite remember when this long card game started. They speculate it began a few years out of college when one of them recognized that enough guys lived in the hometown area to gather for a night of cards. Some knew each other back in grade school, but most met up in high school where their paths crossed through mutual friends, athletics, and music.

In their early years, the poker nights were late, the beer flowed freely, and cigarette smoke filled the air. Nowadays, it's a nine-thirty curfew, decaf fills the mugs, and not an ashtray is in sight. Only the peanut M&Ms and pretzels remain.

And so, of course, does the laughter.

They are merciless teasers. No one in the group is immune, and each man can give as good as he gets. Balding? Point out he's lost a few more hairs. On a diet? Pass him the M&Ms. Stuck with unlucky cards? Raise the ante. They are at their best as the butt of their own jokes, and they like it that way.

Over the years, poker night has been held once a month from September to May in one of the guy's homes. Typically, each wife would hover around to ask what was new with the other wives and children.

Patience has never been the poker group's strong suit.

"Everyone's family fine?" a poker buddy would ask to shorten this process.

"Yep, everybody's good," they'd answer en masse.

The sound of shuffling cards was the cue that it was time to get down to the business of five-card draw.

When poker was at our house, I'd retire with a good book up to my bedroom, which was situated over the dining room. As I lay reading, I'd hear the murmur of their voices, the sound of chips clinking, and the suspenseful silence before baritone belly laughs shook the walls after a well-told joke. This cadence repeated itself throughout the evening until the last hand was dealt and they called it a night.

Their goodbye ritual was always the same. Pushing back their chairs, the boys stretched and yawned as they gathered cards and chips. Slapping each other on the back, they'd head out the door, their farewells ringing throughout the darkness.

"See ya, Andy."

"Night, Banger."

"Take it easy, Fife."

"Thanks, Art."

"Buster's house next month."

And so it would go month after month, year after year. An eclectic mix of aging high school buddies playing poker with pocket change. Like tumbling dice, the decades rolled by. They cheered as each became a father, marveled as their children grew, danced as their children wed, and wondered at the speed of time as grandchildren began to arrive.

And then one day they wept.

On a wintry December morning, just a few weeks after poker night at our house, one of them, perhaps the funniest of the group, died unexpectedly of a heart attack at age fifty-two.

At his funeral, one of the poker guys gave the eulogy and the remaining six were pallbearers. Seven male friends stood together in a church pew with heavy hearts and unabashed tears. Perhaps then, more than ever, they realized the uniqueness of the bond they had inadvertently created through a simple game of cards. Something ordinary had turned into a jackpot.

Since then, the tone of the group has subtly shifted. Perhaps to shed their grief, they sit down to play cards only once or twice a year. Instead, they've cashed in their poker chips for outings, the first of which was a group wellness stop at Heart Check America, a move that saved my husband's life when it was discovered he had 70 percent blockage in his heart.

Once that hurdle was cleared, they shifted into the pursuit of action adventure. They swing golf clubs, rev up the snowmobiles, play basketball, and hit the ballpark. Frequently, they include "their original wives," as they fondly call us, for dinner outings and casual get-togethers and, consequently, despite our own diverse personalities, we are becoming closer as well.

Not long ago, the poker group journeyed to the Northwoods for a snowmobile weekend. Sitting around the fire after a day of sunshine and shadow-lit trails, we coaxed Peter, who usually has a harmonica on hand, to play for us. With finesse and style, he broke into the lilting hymns of "Amazing Grace" and "Simple Gifts."

As the soulful notes filled the air, the room grew still. Only the fire's flames flickered in the cabin's stillness.

In that magical moment, music articulated the unspoken emotions of the group. In the game of life, these high school buddies have been dealt a lucky hand of long, loyal friendship.

The poker pot is priceless.

Hot Time in the Old Town Tonight

I was ten pounds too late. My fortieth high school reunion was upon me and I hadn't lost it. Hadn't dyed the hair, hadn't gotten buff, hadn't won the lottery. Hadn't even drilled up some enthusiasm to go. Even our reunion committee hadn't gotten it together.

Befitting our age, we weren't exactly on the ball, so this was actually the forty-first year since that hot spring day in 1967 when we waltzed out of the gymnasium and into the world with our dreams, some to be realized and, of course, some not.

None of it mattered.

Gratefully, at this point in life, most of us appreciate that a gathering of old friends is more of a come-as-you-are party. And those are the best kind.

By default, having been an officer of my senior class and having moved only five miles upriver from my hometown, I have served as a committee member for our tenth, twentieth, twenty-fifth, thirtieth, and now forty-first reunions, and so over the years I've learned a thing or two about them.

Throw in the fact that every decade since 1965, I've also attended my husband's reunions from the same alma mater, and I am a virtual reunion savant.

Even so, or perhaps for that reason, I just couldn't get my spark back. After forty-one years, what did we really have in common anymore? For many, it's been decades since we've seen each other. Our paths have diverged wildly; we are vastly different people.

And yet, one by one, classmates began to respond, some coming from as far away as both coasts and spending hundreds of dollars to do so. If they could take on all that effort and expense, then I could at least spring for my fifty-five dollars' worth of hors d'oeuvres and show up as well.

As my husband wisely reminded me, "There's always someone that you'll be really glad to see."

Not only was there one, there were many. So, in the spirit of a rah-rah pep song from an old cheerleader, here is a primer of dos and don'ts for an enjoyable reunion experience.

Class, pay attention!

1. TAKE A RISK AND GO. Reunions by nature are tricky business. Some of us have gained weight, lost hair, lost jobs, battled health issues, divorced, or struggled financially. In short, we've experienced life. But reunions should never be about the ones who have done "really, really well."

What does that phrase mean anyway, and who cares? The most money? The biggest house? The most lavish lifestyle? Hardly. Reunions are not about things. They are about people and the delightful discovery that many friendships still run deep after all those years.

So, as Captain Renault said in *Casablanca*, "Round up the usual suspects!"

Be there.

2. MINGLE. This does not mean hang out at the bar with a beer and wait for people to approach you. Muster up some courage and work the room. Extend the glad hand of fellowship. Ask questions. Talk to someone you don't remember or didn't know well.

Some of the best conversations will result.

Even though one classmate and I had gone all the way from grade school through high school together, we both admitted we didn't really remember each other. In a roll call of our elementary teachers, we discovered the only class we ever shared was morning kindergarten. We had a good laugh, and finally, after all these years, got to know each other a bit better.

3. DO NOT LET THE CLIQUES AND BRAGGARTS GET YOU DOWN. Despite your efforts to mix it up, there will always be the few who hang together, talk only about themselves, and never ask about you. It's as if they are the featured guests on *Larry King Live* and you're Larry. On and on they go about what they've achieved, their travels, or the cost of their kid's private school.

To paraphrase the great Wizard of Oz, "Pay no attention!"

Apparently, some people only know how to pontificate about themselves, and after such a one-sided interview, your fun can quickly grind to a halt. Regardless, these classmates always add an interesting mix to the whole experience, so don't take it personally.

As my best friend from kindergarten likes to say, "I've got feet, and I can walk away."

4. SEEK COMMON GROUND. Once you've covered what people have been up to all these years, reconnect with a shared memory. One of my favorite moments came when a classmate greeted me with, "The O's are here!"

Four of us, because our last names began with the letter O, sat next to each other in every class and homeroom we shared in high school, right up to our graduation lineup. We always knew we were in the right place if one or the other of the O's was on either side. His salutation provided that happy reminder.

And as far as the present goes, many of us discovered we had more in common than we thought. We admitted we couldn't hear as well, lacked the energy we used to have, and were taking care of elderly parents, but in our heads at least, still felt like seventeen-year-olds. Sometimes those connections make the best moments and bring the best laughs.

So, find the folks who went to your grade school, belonged to your scout troop, attended your church, or played in your band. You'll not only share some fine memories, but will most likely discover a new person among the old.

5. Be grateful. One of the most poignant moments of my night came when a video displayed the pictures of classmates who had died. I was shocked to see how many were gone. And saddened to see those happy, beaming faces looking out from the pages of our high school yearbook toward all life had to offer. Tragically, their journeys were cut short. And for those of us in attendance, it was a profound reminder that this opportunity to be together was a blessing beyond words. All of those growing-up friendships influenced who we became, who we grew up to be.

The best lesson of the night, however, came from two of our former teachers, one a renowned chemistry instructor and the other an outstanding basketball coach, who graciously took time out of retirement to visit with students from forty years ago. Icons of their era, they epitomized all the values that they had so tirelessly worked to instill in us: honesty, humor, hard work, goodwill, persistence, humility.

We hoped we learned from their examples. For as the popular coach noted, it was unlikely that many of us would ever see each other again, and therefore, what could be more important than making the commitment to revisit old friends?

He was right on target. It was the best reunion I've attended so far. In case you missed yours, here's one final tip:

6. Give an old friend a call. It's never too late. You'll be so glad you did. And next time, be there.

Class dismissed.

Old Friends

We had been young together once.

Now, seated in a dimly lit restaurant almost forty years since our college and newlywed days, the four of us all but failed in our efforts to discreetly observe how the others had aged.

In fact, we could only stare. Our handsome husbands' hair had thinned and silvered, and my brightly smiling sorority sister and I would not be slipping back into our bikinis for a rooftop sunbath anytime soon. Three of us pulled out glasses to read the menu. The fourth already had his on.

Nevertheless, we were joyful to see each other again after almost three decades apart.

"Gosh, you look great!!" we gushed to one another.

And we meant it. After all, we were healthy, happy, and reasonably fit. It's just—how did we get so old so fast?

Weren't we just girls in bell-bottoms with long hair? Weren't the guys just slugging baseballs and running the court offense? Weren't we four newlyweds just staying up way past midnight in a hilarious card game or planning a camping trip out west?

Back then we were young, energetic, and inspired by life's opportunities as we struck out on our own as young adults. But after spending our college and newly married days together, these close friends chose a career move that sent them out east to New Jersey.

Although separated by thousands of miles, our lives continued to follow similar paths. We purchased homes, settled into careers, and raised children born at about the same time. Over the years we kept in touch with Christmas cards and were able to see each other a few times when they returned to Illinois to visit family.

Flash forward thirty years. As we sat and stared at each other over dinner, we all wondered aloud, "Where did the time go?" We found it amazing to think that our children had grown up and moved away. (Two of our children were even married on the same day.) My husband and I were both caring for aging parents, we were soon to be grandparents, and our friends were retired and moving to Nashville.

Retired? Nashville? Fewer taxes there, they explained, which launched us into a discussion of the many new things to think about as we hit our "autumn years."

Though life is good and full of promise, it seems to us that each day is picking up speed, and the world is spinning faster. We see someone in the grocery store with whom we worked on a school or church committee when our kids were growing up, and as we push our cart past and nod hello, we think to ourselves, *Wow, he's aged.* Of course, that person is thinking the same about us. We'd greet him by name, but we can't remember it.

We drive down the street and swerve around some old guy on a bicycle, then realize that "old guy" was in our high school class.

The clerk at the store checks our driver's licenses and reminds us we're eligible for the senior citizen discount.

As the first batch of Baby Boomers to hit retirement age, we marvel that we feel so young inside, while we deal with graying and thinning hair, aging skin, and weight gain on the outside. We try to fight it with exercise, diets, makeup, and hair dye; some take extreme measures like Botox and cosmetic surgery. We even try to proclaim that sixty is the new middle age. Who are we kidding?

Over the centuries, of course, many a poet has lamented the idea of fleeting youth. Perhaps the Psalmist said it most succinctly: "I am but a sojourner on earth." The big question, of course, is: what are we Baby Boomers going to do about the time we have left? Clearly, it's not a time to sit back in a recliner and watch TV. Rather, as the old scout motto goes, it's a time to leave the campground better than we found it.

As our evening with our friends drew to a close, we shared a final laugh over the campground experiences we shared on the crazy trip to the West Coast we'd taken together in our early twenties.

Although we thought we were well prepared, much went wrong. In our youthful naïveté, we had crossed the desert with no water, traveled on a penniless budget, slept in borrowed canvas Boy Scout tents with no floors, snuggled in sleeping bags not warm enough for frigid mountain air, brought a Coleman stove that we could never get to work, and had our car broken into when we went off sightseeing.

Yet looking back, what a joyous adventure it had been. Because our cameras were stolen, we have few pictures of that trip. But I still remember the night we camped on the pine-scented slope of Mount Rainier and watched as, one by one, the golden glow of other campers' fires lit the forest like a string of mountain fireflies.

Someday, I'd like to repeat that trip. (Maybe in a pop-up camper this time.) But in the meantime, I'll cherish these lifelong friends, the memories we've shared, and the opportunities to keep in touch no matter how many miles separate us.

Thankfully, some small measure of wisdom accompanies the aging process and, with it, the realization that lifelong friendships are beautiful gifts. Despite the busy nature of life, it is worth every effort to keep them going.

For when we do, at least for one fleeting moment in time, our hearts feel young again.

Comfort and Joy

The smell in the bone marrow transplant wing is unsettling. Three close friends holed up in the dim and dreary isolation room of a teaching hospital try unsuccessfully to ignore it.

Two of the women are in visitors' chairs; the third sits propped up on a bed as mega-doses of chemotherapy drugs drip into her veins. It is two days before Christmas, but we are not merry.

Ravaged by breast cancer, Nancy has already endured a mastectomy, radiation, and six months of chemotherapy. Because the cancer has infiltrated her lymph nodes, she has chosen to undergo a risky experimental bone marrow transplant that she hopes will provide a cure.

Once a striking woman with thick, raven hair, a petite figure, and an energetic smile, she now lies bald and listless on the bed, her body puffy, her skin covered with the beginnings of an angry purple rash.

Just a week ago, the three of us sat in Nancy's cozy living room, enjoying drinks, hors d'oeuvres, and lively conversation with our husbands. The room was filled with the soft light of the fireplace and the glow of the Christmas tree. We were all dressed in festive attire and, despite her wig and pale skin, Nancy looked radiant. Blocking the upcoming hospital ordeal from our minds as best we could, we all concentrated on sharing a wonderful evening together.

But now the Christmas future we held at bay that night is upon us, and Jan and I sit awkwardly in the bleak isolation room trying to think of pleasant things to say. Shocked by Nancy's appearance, we try to make light of our own. In deference to Nancy's weakened immune system, we are sheathed in sterile hospital gowns, booties, gloves, and masks. We look silly, for sure, but our attempts at humor are weak and uninspired. Beneath our masks, we grow hot and sweaty.

Jan is Nancy's longtime neighbor, and I am Nancy's childhood friend from Sunday school. As second-graders, we received our Bibles together on a warm June morning in 1954. Although Nancy moved away in sixth grade, our paths crossed again some twenty years later when we ended up joining the same church as young mothers in a different town.

Who would have guessed back then that our paths would lead to this place?

Desperate to make conversation, Jan and I discuss our Christmas plans, which visiting relatives are driving us crazy, our dinner menus for Christmas Day, the hectic last-minute shopping and wrapping still left to do.

To Nancy, of course, all this is meaningless. Her Christmas plans are the same as today's: more chemo, more nausea, more depressing isolation. I wonder if we are only making her feel worse. But she maintains a stoic and cheerful interest in our Christmas chatter.

Suddenly, Nancy politely excuses herself and vomits the remains of her lunch into a bedside pan. Ever the gracious hostess, her immediate concern is not her own comfort or embarrassment but the possibility that her guests may be sickened by the sight.

Apologizing, she tries to clean herself up. Jan assists with tissues and sips of water while I stand helplessly at the foot of her bed, numbly patting her foot.

Too soon, we are reminded by the fading gray light coming through the room's single window that it is time to go: Jan and I back to the warmth and love of family Christmas celebrations, Nancy to her solitary suffering and an unknown future.

Rising to leave, Jan and I fumble awkwardly over parting words. Guilt over our own good health and waiting families makes "Merry Christmas" sound so hollow. How can we even say it? Should we?

Suddenly, the tension is too much. Nancy, who normally keeps her emotions very private, begins to sob. It's a merciful release, and abruptly Jan and I break down as well, finally relaxing as warm tears soak our paper masks. I realize that, although we are the best of friends, we have never seen each other cry.

In a season of holiday giving, in a room where worldly presents are neither allowed nor useful, the only gifts we can offer are those that flow unbidden from our hearts. Normally unspoken words of love, encouragement, and hope now pour forth spontaneously, suffusing the room like soothing music.

"We love you, Nancy."

"You're hanging in there so well."

"I'll be praying for you every day."

Truthful, simple words. The only gifts we have.

Finally, we move toward the door. We do not say goodbye, just "Merry Christmas." It doesn't sound hollow at all.

～

In loving memory of Nancy Lee Sayers, 1949–1998

Windy Day Wreckage

No one stopped. The wind howled across the open prairie as we surveyed the damage. It blew the dirt into gray mists of dust. It rocked our truck, already parked at a listing angle on the side of a gravel ditch. It snapped at our hair, clothes, and bodies with such strength that we struggled to keep our balance.

Before us lay shards of broken glass and the upside-down remains of a 1930s Amish oak-and-pine bookcase we had just purchased from a dealer at a country antique show.

For some time, I'd been looking for just the right bookcase for my writing studio in hopes that something big and serviceable would combat my lack of organizational skills. Finally, I'd found it.

On this beautiful spring morning with green, fuchsia, and yellow flowers sprinkled across the farmlands like confetti, my husband and I had driven across country roads in eager anticipation of the year's first outdoor antique market.

After a long, cold winter, we were looking forward to strolling beneath the ancient oaks that lined the fairgrounds and browsing in the sunshine and warm breeze as we made our search. For us, a day at an outdoor antique market is like a day at an art museum with nature as its backdrop.

Ambling past a variety of booths, we scanned the merchandise for pieces that might serve as a bookcase; buffets, china cabinets, and, of course, actual bookcases were all possibilities. Yet, as in

"Goldilocks and the Three Bears," some were too big, some too small, and some were just not practical enough, lovely as they were.

We headed over to a dealer from whom we had purchased several unique items in the past in hopes that his winter searches might have turned up something interesting. They had. Sequestered at the back of his tent stood a charming four-shelf cabinet with three deep drawers in its base. The dealer told us it came from an Amish kitchen, and it was easy to surmise that the bottom bins might have been used to store flour, sugar, or other goods.

The imposing five-by-seven-foot frame was made of quarter-sawn oak and the shelves and backing of plain pine. The Amish tend to use or recycle whatever wood is at hand, and the contrasting, patchwork result looked beautiful and strong.

I loved the original silver-toned handles that opened the cabinet's glass doors, and I didn't mind a variety of water stains on the shelves. They added character and hinted intriguingly at the cabinet's past life. A narrow shelf separated the cabinet on top from the bins below—a perfect ledge for my work. The dealer had recently refinished the entire piece to a beautiful patina, and, without looking any further, we both knew it would be perfect for my writing studio.

We asked for his best price. He came down a bit. We countered. He recountered. Sold.

Handing him a still-significant check, we said we'd be back in a bit to load up. The day was early, lovely, and warm, and we wanted to scout around awhile, intrigued by what else might be out there.

As we sauntered down the lanes lined with antiques, we couldn't believe our good fortune at finding want I'd wanted so early. It was my lucky day.

Suddenly, the sound of breaking glass caught our attention.

"Boy, it's getting windy!" I said.

"Looks like the booth over there just lost a whole shelf of cookie jars," my husband answered.

Heading back, we once again heard the crash of glass and watched as dealers scrambled to secure their treasures. The wind was increasing.

My husband retrieved our truck and met me back at the bookcase booth. Separating the top half of the cabinet from its base, my husband and the dealer struggled to lift and wedge the two heavy pieces into the back end of the truck. Having secured the two pieces tightly together with a strong rope, we felt we were safely on our way.

But back out on the country roads, surrounded by freshly plowed open fields, it didn't take us long to notice that the brisk breeze had escalated to a wild wind, and then to a raging gale. Having been protected by the trees and buildings at the fairgrounds, we were shocked at its sudden force.

Looking back at the top half of the bookcase, I was dismayed to see that it had swayed and shifted.

"It's OK," my husband reassured me. "The base and top are tied firmly together, and they're both really heavy. It's not going anywhere."

Nevertheless, he slowed the truck down from an already cautious speed. The wind blew straight across the truck's side like the breath of a giant. We were miles from our turnoff with no relief in sight.

With the bookcase angled back across the base, I scanned the horizon for anything that could break the wind. We passed a farmhouse and barn that offered momentary relief, but as soon as we were back in the open, the wind punched us with ferocity.

"There it goes!" my husband suddenly shouted. "I can't believe it!"

Turning to look, I watched in disbelief. As if in slow motion, the cabinet slipped out of its ropes, flipped up into the air, and with a bounce landed upside down in a steep roadside ditch.

I won't repeat the swear words.

We pulled off the road and jumped out of the truck to survey the damage.

Holding my breath, I approached the wreckage. I told myself if the three glass doors were broken, they could be easily fixed. They were. Large shards of glass were everywhere.

Since it was lying on its front, I hoped that the rest would not be so damaged.

"Let's see if we can flip it over," my husband said.

Pushing against the gale, we struggled to get a grip and maintain our footing on the steep grassy slope. As we lifted the bookcase up, it was plain to see that much more than the glass had broken.

The original silver-toned handles were ripped off or smashed, the framework was split apart and busted, the beautiful oak was gouged with deep scratches from the shoulder's gravel, and grass protruded from the cracked woodwork like fanciful decorations.

I was too shocked to cry. Most people would have cut their losses and abandoned the wreck on the side of the road. But with amazing optimism, my husband suggested we try to load the remains back into the truck.

In a matter of seconds, my chagrin over the bookcase turned to true terror as car after car whizzed within inches of my husband as we wrestled with the wreckage. Together, we struggled to hold the heavy piece together while lifting it on the slippery slope. There was the distinct possibility of me falling back onto the huge chunks of glass or my husband getting hit by a car. Using every muscle in our bodies, we finally maneuvered our wreck back into the truck.

Standing on the fender to help resecure the behemoth, I suddenly heard peals of gut-busting laughter. I glanced in the truck's open window to see if we'd left the radio on in our hurry to retrieve the bookcase, but everything was off. Baffled, I scanned the horizon, and my eyes caught sight of the farmhouse we had passed earlier about one hundred yards away. There in the driveway stood three big burly men beside their ATVs, looking our way and laughing their heads off. Even with the roar of the wind, I could hear their boisterous belly laughs, which continued for the duration of our struggles.

It was like a laugh track from an old TV show that just wouldn't turn off.

Driving at a snail's pace, we made the precarious journey home. My new fear was that the shredded remains would somehow escape the ropes once more and hit one of the many cars that were now following slowly in our wake. Worse than injuring ourselves was the horrific possibility that we could inadvertently injure someone else. Add to that thoughts of being sued for all our worth and spending the rest of our lives in jail, and I was living one big nightmare.

At last, we arrived home safely. Our driveway never looked so good.

With a flurry of effort and thirty-six years of the Reader's Digest *Do-It-Yourself* book under his belt, my husband set about putting the mess together again.

He sanded. He stained. He varnished. He glued. He measured for new glass. He hunted for matching handles. He filled cracks. He nailed. And unlike Humpty Dumpty, he succeeded.

As I write this, a lovely re-refinished Amish bookcase stands regally to my right. You'd never know it had been retrieved, shattered, from a ditch. Any subtle scratches or nicks that might remain (and you'd have to look closely to find them) are like laugh lines on a face—they only add character and history.

The bookcase reminds me that my husband's actions speak volumes of love; that many things that seem hopeless are not; that in the scheme of life, earthly possessions are meaningless; and that missed chances to help one another are missed moments of grace.

Sometimes, when I replace a book behind the cabinet's re-glued and revarnished doors, a piece of ditch gravel will tumble from some unknown crevice. And then, I can't help but stand back and laugh at the miracle. All of them.

Guys? Can you hear me over the wind?

Blest Be the Ties That Bind

Grief can take care of itself, but to get the full value of joy you must have somebody to divide it with.

—Mark Twain

Dance Lessons

It was dark when I bolted out the door of the dance club. Darker than I thought. Colder than I thought. But I was steamed, really steamed, and there was no stopping me.

I had taken just enough time to grab my coat before I made my exit, which was a good thing. The frigid night air whacked me in the face.

Some unknown Chicago street stretched out before me, lit only by the glow of infrequent streetlights and the ice-covered red of taillights passing by. If not the cold, the darkness, or the unfamiliarity of my surroundings, common sense should have stopped me. It did not.

I was outta there. These legs, these tapping toes, were not going to sit on the sidelines of the dance floor for one more minute. They were takin' a walk.

And baby, that's exactly what they did. Like a steam engine flashing sparks, I hit the track. It was seven long city blocks in two-inch heels before my husband and his buddy caught up with me.

"What's wrong?" my husband asked with the care of someone defusing a bomb.

"I'm tired of watching everyone else dance fast," I answered, the subzero temperature having exhausted my anger to a smolder.

The two men, best friends from high school, nodded sagely, instinctively knowing further conversation was fruitless. The three of us traveled the long walk back in silence.

The rest of our party, being the lifelong friends that they are, pretended as though nothing unusual had occurred. The festive atmosphere of our rare night out for dinner and dancing, however, lost its warmth when I blew back in the door. It wasn't long before we were putting on our coats and heading home to pay the babysitters for fewer hours than they had anticipated. I take full blame for throwing ice on that good time.

Although this angry winter walk occurred long ago, it still stands out in my mind because not only did I act foolishly but also, in nearly thirty-five years of marriage, it remains our most significant (and public) eruption. All because my husband wouldn't dance fast.

I have always loved to dance. My husband has not.

As high school sweethearts shuffling around the gymnasium floor draped in each other's arms during the mid-1960s, our dancing differences didn't matter much.

Through the years of our married life, when the tunes turned fast at a wedding reception, business party, or philanthropic event, we'd head to the sidelines, content to visit with friends or grab some refreshments. When the slow music came on at these occasions, we both meandered to the dance floor for our old cheek-to-cheek two-step, but it was the fast dances that continued to sideline us. I began to feel like a benched basketball player watching all the fun and action on the court. My feet itched to be out there.

Over the years, to my husband's credit, he occasionally (albeit reluctantly) tried to dance fast. And although he is a standout athlete and musician, gyrating beside me on the dance floor made him feel like a cork bobbing aimlessly in a windless sea.

"Just move to the music," I'd say.

"This is stupid," he'd respond.

As a result, over the decades we've not danced together to the twist, the monkey, the swim, the holly golly, the disco dancing of the 1980s, or the macarena of the 1990s. Don't even mention the "YMCA." Some would say that we haven't missed much, but I guess on that frigid Chicago night, my inner-dancer had had enough.

It wasn't until the upcoming marriage of our oldest son, nearly three years ago, that my husband decided to take action. The thought of having to dance in front of over two hundred people must have produced a cold sweat.

"We need to take some dance lessons," he casually mentioned several months before the wedding.

To say my chair virtually tipped over backward is an understatement.

"Why?" I asked in astonishment.

"Well, we're going to have to dance at the wedding," he said. "And I don't like doing things I can't do well."

"OK," I answered, refraining from jumping into midair and executing a jubilant John Travolta spin.

To my further surprise, he'd already done the research and checked out available lessons at a local community college. By the next day we were signed up.

To my delight, my husband took to the dance lessons like Sammy Sosa to a corked bat. He had found his groove. Here was something that made sense to him: counting and actual steps, not just mindless shaking on the dance floor. Our dancing began to take shape. Frank Sinatra and Glenn Miller became our new best friends.

Amazingly, and before we knew it, we were cruisin' around the dance floor. "Rock step, slow-slow, rock step, slow-slow" was our mantra. As the weekly lessons went by, we were not only doing the steps but actually adding turns, twirls, and twists. Besides the swing, our repertoire included the waltz and the fox trot. Our dancing confidence climbed.

After a midlesson break, my husband was the first on the dance floor when the music started up again, dragging this exhausted wife with him. At home we'd practice, practice, practice. Round and round the dining room table and across the kitchen floor we'd go, me in faded robe and slippers, he in jeans and flannel.

"Slow, quick-quick, slow," we muttered in time with the beat. We'd circle the porch pool table to the tunes of "Chattanooga Choo Choo" and "Tuxedo Junction." We'd cruise past the coffee table to "Stardust" and "In the Mood." On occasion, we had to pull out our cheat sheet to remember the steps, but on we danced.

Knowing that Dave Matthews, not the Big Band sound of the 1940s, was likely to rule at our son's reception, we tried more modern musicians and were delighted to discover that our new dance steps (depending on the tempo and the count) worked just fine. We could rock step to the Beach Boys and fox trot to the Beatles. We were set. Or so we thought.

After a beautiful wedding, we found ourselves confused by the DJ's mix of music at the reception (even the "Anniversary Waltz" was not a waltz). We couldn't find our beat, but our son, his new bride, and all their energetic friends did, packing the dance floor and dancing joyously the whole night through.

For once, I was content to watch all that happiness from the sidelines.

Other dancing occasions have come our way, however, and despite a few nervous flutters at the start, we've gotten up and out there. Sometimes, in fact, we are the only ones on the dance floor, which makes us feel a little like Fred and Ginger, until one of us stumbles. Then we simply stop, laugh, whisper the beat to each other, and start over. The sidelines are no longer part of our dance card.

As our second son's wedding draws near, we will start our practice regimen again. He and his fiancée favor jazz, so perhaps we'll try a little improvisation to Wynton Marsalis. Who knows? If all else fails, we can always revert to our old standby: a slow, shapeless shuffle across the dance floor, arms around each other, cheek to cheek.

I have to admit, it's still the best.

Mission Impossible

Our hair was long and our skirts were short. We were the first generation to wear miniskirts. Striding around campus, we strutted our stuff in knee-high boots and platform sandals. We were lean and hip and we had attitude.

And now, alas, the fashion industry has passed us by. Like a forgotten dress hanging faded and limp in the back of the closet, we middle-aged moms with children of marrying age cannot for the life us find dresses for their weddings.

With the spring and summer wedding seasons approaching, millions of formerly miniskirted women are now scrambling through every department store, mall, or boutique known to womankind, like a bevy of buzzing bees searching frantically for the perfect flower.

"Have you found your dress?" we ask each other at work, the grocery store, the post office.

"Have you found your dress?" ask our friends, our family members, our dentists.

The answer is a resounding no!

As mothers of the brides and grooms, we have high hopes. We want to look good gliding down that aisle on the arm of a handsome son or childhood friend.

After the beautiful bride and lovely bridesmaids, we'd like to hold our own. These are joyous moments for our children, and we want to shine right along with them.

Listen up, fashion industry! Is that too much to ask?

Yes, we admit, these many years later, time and gravity are taking their toll. Our skirts are longer, our hair shorter, and most of the time we wear sensible shoes.

But does that mean we have to look like duds?

Yes, it is true, the tummies that produced those beautiful babies are a bit rounder, the arms that hauled thirty-pound toddlers for hours on end are not so toned, and the faces that peered through a window searching the darkness for a teenager returning home safely are a bit more lined. But we are not down for the count. We're up and swinging and trying to hold it all together (so to speak).

This is my second time attempting the nightmarish hunt for a wedding dress. Three years ago, I made my dress hunt debut when my first son was married. I searched high and low, crossed field and dale, forded streams and climbed mountains. In a moment of desperation, I succumbed to an incredibly svelte, twenty-something saleswoman's pitch that I looked "fabulous!" in a beige, satin, spaghetti-strap dress in a size smaller than I normally wear. To add to the duplicity, the store used those trick mirrors you find at the circus that make you look twenty pounds thinner and a foot taller.

"Not bad," I thought to myself. "I'll take it."

Doubling the national debt, I paid the piper, took it home, and hung it in my closet until ten days before the wedding, when I decided to try it on again.

Horrors of horrors! I looked twenty pounds heavier and a foot shorter. Sleek and slim, I was not! Honey, it would take the grip of an industrial strength girdle to hold this gut in for ten hours of wedding and reception.

What had I been thinking?

Out I raced like a mouse after the last piece of cheese on earth, scurrying through rack after rack of drab and dowdy mother-of-the-bride/groom dresses until, miracles of miracles, I found a lovely, blue floral silk with a pretty neckline and matching shawl. With a few minor alterations, it was ready to go two days before the wedding.

Not wanting to repeat that scenario, I started looking earlier (one would think four months' lead time was enough) for my second son's upcoming wedding. On the pretense of celebrating my husband's birthday, I dragged the dear man into Chicago for a hike up Michigan Avenue, figuring a second trusted opinion would save me from my past mistakes.

We started our search in the dress department of a well-known store, assuming they would surely have a vast selection. As my husband and I began wandering through the racks, I became increasingly dismayed.

"See what I mean," I said. "There's nothing here."

Like the knight in shining armor that he is, my husband attempted to come to his lady's rescue (because his lady was getting grumpier by the moment).

"Where would we find the mother-of-the-bride or -groom dresses?" my husband innocently asked an incredibly svelte salesclerk as we stood in the middle of a long aisle surrounded by hundreds of dresses.

"Well, any of these would work," the incredibly svelte salesclerk answered, as though we were a pair of blind bats.

"Well, how about something for someone her age?" my prince suggested. (I'm not taking him again.)

"Just look around," the incredibly svelte salesclerk said.

And so we did.

If I was going to prom, the dresses to my left would have been perfect: slinky, strapless numbers with no backs and bunches of what I can only describe as foofoo shooting out from the butt and bust in iridescent shades of orange, limeade, and raspberry that would have blinded a possum at night.

If I was going to a fancy funeral, the dresses to my right would have been just the ticket: long, shapeless jackets over long, shapeless dresses with strangle-hold necklines in deathlike tones of smog gray, dirt brown, burnished black, and, that perennial fashion industry joke, the ever-present milquetoast beige. To add insult to injury, for what one of these novelties cost we could have made a down payment on a car.

Suddenly the absurdity of it all struck a funny bone, and we started to laugh.

"How about this one?" my husband asked, gesturing to a satin sack the color of mud.

"Or this?" I countered, seductively winking from behind a blazing yellow tube of a gown that could be worn at auditions for Ms. Chiquita Banana.

It was all great for a good chuckle except for the sobering fact that I still needed a dress.

Out the door we bolted, a pair of old fogies on a scavenger hunt, zigzagging up Michigan Avenue into one boutique and out of another. Nada, nada, nada. It was all the same.

Finally, we rested in the lounge of a favorite hotel, ordered a drink, and took inventory of my choices. My husband's only comment was that his birthday beer never tasted so good.

Back home, I made the usual rounds through local stores and boutiques with the same results.

"Oh, most mothers with summer weddings have already purchased their dresses," snipped one salesclerk. "This is all we have left."

Silly me. It was already February!

One evening, I poured out my dress dilemma to a valued friend and longtime neighbor. "Do I go to my son's wedding as a thirty-something wannabe, or do I go for safe and dowdy in a grandma gown?" I asked.

In a nanosecond she replied, "I'd err on the side of a thirty-something wannabe." This from a seventy-something grandma. With attitude.

And so, girls, I'm going for it. I have found a lovely spaghetti-strap dress in a size smaller than I normally wear. I have a shawl. And I have replaced all the mirrors in my house with the ones you find at the circus.

I would describe the dress in more detail to you, but, alas, it's just about time to start my new daily routine of two hundred sit-ups, fifty-pound weight lifting for the arms, and my five-mile walk. Then it's on to a lunch with no salt, mayo, cheese, sugar, butter, et cetera.

Middle-aged bridal mothers, unite! Throw off the bonds of dowdy and dull and alert the fashion industry to our revolt!

We aren't asking for much! Just pretty colors that aren't so dark or washed out that we look like death warmed over, a little sex appeal in the neckline or hem, the suggestion that we still have waists, and a few fashion details that camouflage you-know-what, and we'd be happy.

Throw in a reasonable price tag that doesn't require taking out a second mortgage on the house, and wedding celebrations everywhere will be filled with moms strutting down that aisle happy, hip, and with a just a smidge of attitude.

After all, our dear and blessed children, it's your glorious day, and we'd be there in rags if necessary.

For you, we'd even wear miniskirts.

Language of Love

They spoke almost no English. Journeying from the biblical vistas of Mount Ararat, they flew thousands of miles across the cities of Europe, the blue-green swells of the Atlantic Ocean, and the drought-dried fields of America's heartland before arriving in the hot concrete jungle of the distinctly different Dallas.

Hamlet and Karine (Kara) traveled all this way bearing gifts of cognac and handmade pillow covers from their native Armenia to celebrate their daughter's wedding to my nephew.

It was my fifth wedding of the summer, which started with my own son's celebration with his beautiful high school sweetheart and would conclude with our nephew's long-awaited marriage to his Armenian bride. In between were the wonderful weddings of friends.

Each celebration reflected not only the unique love of the bride and groom but also the parents' love for their children. For, although they are times of great happiness, weddings also represent a time of separation as our children journey forth with their beloved partners and create lives of their own.

They go, of course, with our blessings but not without a soft sigh from our hearts as we realize that our children are now grown and belong to someone else.

We parents try to be subtle about this letting go, but we are not so good at it.

I witnessed this in a myriad of undisguised moments during each summer wedding: the emotional struggle in a dad's voice as he delivered a humorous and heartfelt toast at a rehearsal dinner; a mother's sweet, prolonged adjustment of her son's tuxedo tie as they waited for the ceremony to begin; and a father's tender kisses on his daughter's forehead as they lovingly danced at a reception.

Such small moments are wordless expressions of the deep, ever-flowing love a parent has for a child. And although we parents try to keep these powerful emotions under wraps, they bubble up at unexpected moments.

So my heart went out to Hamlet and Kara, who were not simply celebrating their only daughter's wedding in a foreign land but also adjusting to their first trip to America. Besides not knowing the language, they had to handle the heavy heat of Dallas, the congested traffic, the Tex-Mex food, and the ongoing introductions to yet another set of family members who kept appearing on the scene. In addition, as the bride's parents, they had an important role to play.

But none of that seemed to affect Hamlet's or Kara's demeanor. Kara's lovely smile and sparkling eyes spoke volumes, and she knew a smattering of words like *beautiful* and *good* and *thank you*, which, when you think about it, cover a lot of territory.

Hamlet displayed a quiet dignity that overshadowed what must have been tremendous culture shock. Although he knew no English, he was not afraid to venture forth in his own language, translated by the bride's two Armenian girlfriends. (After all, the bride, who speaks impeccable English, could hardly be expected to translate her father's toast to herself.)

"Shhhh! Hamlet is going to speak!" someone would announce throughout the weekend celebrations. And then Hamlet would take center stage, gather his thoughts, and confidently deliver a toast in his musical native tongue.

"He says, 'We parents are like gardeners, and these are our flowers,'" the young Armenian woman translated for the groom's parents. "'We have raised and nurtured our flowers separately, but now these beautiful flowers will bloom together.'"

Gathered guests nodded in perfect understanding.

"He wants to know if the vows included honoring one another in sickness and health, in good times and bad?" the young interpreter asked the bride and groom, who confirmed that this was so. Satisfied, Hamlet carried on.

"He wishes that you love each other always," the interpreter continued. "'May you share one pillow as you go through life and grow old together. When you have difficulties, and you will, for life is hard, your love can overcome these obstacles. Your love will see you through.'"

Although we did not know much of Hamlet's personal background, it was clear he knew of what he spoke.

Earlier in the day, with the morning shadows still cooling the wedding venue's backyard garden, Hamlet stood poised in his American tuxedo with his radiant daughter on his arm. To the sounds of a lush brass quintet, they started down the grassy aisle together.

This is always one of the most poignant moments of a wedding for me. Even if I don't know the family well, emotion wells up within me, like water ready to burst a dam. It takes all my strength to keep from breaking into sobs.

I can only attribute these emotions to the memory of my father and the deep love I felt as we began our walk down the aisle at my wedding decades ago. I was only twenty, and at the end of the aisle waiting for me was a man my father loved and respected and I adored (still do).

Perhaps it is because my father died a mere six years later that this moment, a time to leave and a time to join together, holds such a cherished place in my heart.

And so I felt a special empathy for this Armenian father as he listened and watched an entire ceremony spoken in words that held no meaning for him. What could be going through his head as his daughter not only left his family to join another's but also adopted a new culture and country?

As the bride and groom concluded their vows with a kiss and began their walk back down the garden path to the music of the quintet and to a new life of their own, Hamlet suddenly shouted out in his native Armenian to his once-little girl.

"Be happy!" he said in a loud, clear voice. "Happiness to you always!"

The universal language of a parent's heart.

No interpretation needed.

❧

Hamlet and his daughter, Anna, were never to see each other again. Tragically, two years later, Hamlet Charchoghlyan was killed in a head-on car crash with a truck on the curve of an Armenian mountain road. May he rest in peace.

Making of a Mother-in-Law

The mother-in-law muse is very powerful. Like the muse of poetry, who provides writers with verbal inspiration, this muse provides mothers-in-law with opinions, and lots of them.

"Do it my way" might be a mother-in-law's musical mantra in a revised version of the old Frank Sinatra standard, especially when she feels compelled to pass her muse-inspired advice on to an unsuspecting daughter-in-law.

As a novice mother-in-law of two years with another daughter-in-law soon to join the ranks, I've come to the conclusion that "the muse made me say it" is the only logical explanation for my need to share my worldly wisdom with these young women.

One only needs to read daily advice columns to see the mother-in-law cast as a constant culprit, stirring up marital trouble between her daughter-in-law and her son. No wonder the old adage to the mother of the groom is, "Wear beige and shut up."

Unfortunately, I look like a bowl of cold oatmeal in beige, and shutting up is not one of my strengths.

If not the muse, what is it that makes a mother-in-law want to voice her opinions so frequently? I can only use the excuse my three boys gave while burping like a bevy of bullfrogs at the dinner table when they were young.

"We can't help it!" they'd giggle together after I admonished them.

A chorus of more and louder burps would follow just to prove their point.

As an excuse, however, this doesn't hold much air (forgive the pun). So, in an attempt to avoid being the lead story in an advice column, I often ponder the pitfalls that pepper so many mother-in-law/daughter-in-law relationships.

Thankfully, I need go no further than my husband's wonderful eighty-seven-year-old mother, who presents a prime example of what a mother-in-law should be. In all my years of marriage, she has never criticized me or offered advice unless I asked for her opinion. Over the years, there have been no suggestions on how to raise my children, cook for my husband, keep house, or alter a career. And those are just the big issues.

No matter how important or insignificant the circumstances, she has refrained from verbally judging me. And that is no small accomplishment. Although I have always appreciated her efforts, not until I became a mother-in-law myself did I realize that such a stance doesn't necessarily come naturally or without a lot of work.

So at a recent family outing, I told my mother-in-law how grateful I was not only for her approach but also for setting an example for me. Without hesitation, my sister-in-law seconded my thoughts, and I'm sure if our third sister-in-law had been there, she would have agreed in the blink of an eye as well.

Although the three of us are as different as can be, our mother-in-law has always treated us equally, which attests to her gifts of noninterference and tolerance.

"It couldn't have been easy, though," I said.

"No," she answered honestly and with a smile. "It wasn't."

(My sister-in-law and I looked at each other in horror. What? We weren't perfect?)

"I'm finding that keeping my mouth shut is no easy task," I confided, as my mother-in-law nodded in agreement. "So, the fact that you have been able to do so all these years shows amazing fortitude."

Raising our glasses, we all (her two sons included) toasted my mother-in-law for this achievement.

Yet, as I tread down my own mother-in-law road, I'm discovering that even with the best intentions in mind, it is easy to end up putting one's foot in one's mouth, or in my case, foot in one's pants.

Not long ago, my daughter-in-law called to say she had stopped by the dry cleaners to pick up some pants, but the cleaners had inadvertently sent them home with my husband's shirts. Had I seen them?

"Are they black Capri style?' I asked.

"Yes."

"Little slits on the side?"

"Yes."

"Side zip?"

"Yes."

"Well, I have good news," I said, bursting out laughing. "Not only have I seen them, I'm wearing them! In fact, I've been wearing them all week!"

"Oh no!" she said. And because she is a wise and wonderful daughter-in-law, she laughed too.

"They're really nice pants," I tried to explain. "I'd wondered why I hadn't worn them for a while. I guess it's because they're yours!"

I quickly apologized and offered to have them dry-cleaned again. Later in the week, I hung them on her back door with a note that read, "I promise never to wear your pants again." We both had a good laugh over it, but when I told my second son, who was soon to be married, he looked at me warily and didn't laugh so hard.

"That's pretty bad, Mom," he said. "Couldn't you tell they weren't yours?"

"Well, no," I said, sheepishly. "I just thought I'd forgotten about them."

I think he later advised his bride-to-be to hide her clothes and not use his mother's cleaners once they were married.

As the mother of three sons, my mother-in-law likes to say she got her daughters all grown up. As another mother of three sons, I will do the same. And what a wonderful gift. Strong, bright young women, who are taking flight like beautiful butterflies with hopes and dreams of their own.

No matter what the mother-in-law muse says, it is not my job to steer their courses, but rather to enjoy and learn from the paths they choose. And in the process, I hope I can be whatever they need: a mother, a woman, a friend.

My mother-in-law recently told her grandson, after his engagement celebration, "I know you would only choose the very best." What a wonderful demonstration of acceptance to him, and for me, another example of superb mother-in-law mentoring.

Of course, being prejudiced, I think my new girls chose pretty well themselves, and as long as they don't ask me to wear beige, I think I can keep my mouth shut. At least I'll try.

Which means, girls, you're on your own with the burping business.

Christmas Windows

The windows beckon. And as usual, we're running late. Our early morning train leaves in twenty minutes, and the station is at least a ten-minute drive away, plus parking.

The panic begins to set in. Where are my shoes? Do you have a hat? Don't forget a scarf!

Our race to the train station gets our hearts pumping, not to mention the sweat. With minutes to spare, we climb the stairs to the train's upper deck, breathing big sighs of relief and scrambling for seats that give us a good view of the river and passing countryside. A couple "choo choos" (usually from me) and we're on our way.

For twenty-seven years, we've been making this train trek into Chicago to see the Marshall Field's windows the day after Thanksgiving.

"Are you nuts?" our friends politely ask us. "Why would you go Christmas shopping there on the busiest day of the year?"

"Oh, we never shop," I answer. "We just enjoy the windows and the ambiance."

More incredulous stares.

How do I explain the desire to brave crowds, questionable weather, and long waits? Part of the allure is the walk. Even when our three boys were babies, we hiked the long city blocks from Chicago's train depot to Marshall Field's, hauling strollers, diaper bags, and toddlers. The burst of cold air after the warmth of the train car invigorated us as we set off at a fast clip into the Windy City.

Zigzagging through the streets, we crossed Daley Plaza, admired the gigantic live Christmas tree, watched the miniature train run its course, and breathed in the pungent scent of sauerkraut from the German shops.

Then it was on to State Street with the first order of the day: viewing Field's windows, which had a new theme every year. Starting at the far northwest corner of the store, we worked our way down the street and along the storyline, admiring the colorful details of each display. Before the boys could read, I recited the narratives to them, much to the chagrin or gratitude of those around me. (It is a habit I still can't shake, even though my boys now hover around six feet tall.)

Moving gingerly through the crowd, we not only absorbed the window displays but also took in the wonder of the sights around us: the Salvation Army bell-ringers with their silver horns, the fanfare of giant golden trumpets protruding high above us into the sparkling white lights of the trees, the strains of street musicians' sweet violins or sassy saxophones, and the burnished patina of Field's green clock under which we were to meet if we ever became separated.

The best windows, in my humble opinion, were the ones that actually depicted Christmas. Scrooge and Tiny Tim top my list, with Dickens's timeless message of the season. The display of Chicago Christmases over the decades, with its lovely family scenes, added an intriguing historical element. And the *Nutcracker Suite* always established a mood of magic and enchantment.

I can't say Harry Potter, Cinderella, or Snow White stoked my Yuletide fires. Nevertheless, the Field's windows always gave us a good opportunity for analysis and observation.

In the early years, with our window promenade complete, it was on to see the Field's Santa. Swinging through the revolving doors into the engulfing warmth and sweetness of the perfume section, we made a beeline to the North Pole.

This involved no simple ride up the escalator. Our system included a series of ruses that would challenge any detective. Consequently, we were usually the first ones in line to see Santa Claus.

I can still see our first visit to Santa with my eighteen-month-old son standing sweetly before him, dressed in his little red plaid pants and matching handmade sweater, and our last visit sixteen years later when Santa cheerily greeted this now-tall seventeen-year-old by reading the name scripted on his high school jacket.

"Why, hello, John!" he intoned in his deep, Santa voice. "My, how you have grown!"

We all had a good laugh, but knew it was time to check Santa off our to-do list for good. Just for fun and old time's sake, we occasionally go by and wave.

Because of that early morning train, we would all be starving after seeing Santa. In the early years, we endured the long wait to eat in the Walnut Room near the Christmas tree before we discovered a fast little cafeteria on the eighth floor that served the same food and offered a glimpse of Lake Michigan and the surrounding buildings. Much more manageable for three hungry boys and their parents.

With our mission accomplished, we usually headed home on the 12:40 p.m. train. But as the boys grew, we started to extend our stay, hiking up Michigan Avenue not only to check out the sights and the action but also to find good burgers and fries.

Over the years, our sojourn sometimes included a stop at the Art Institute to admire the wreathed lions and take in the nativity art before trekking the entire distance to the north end of the Magnificent Mile. Comfortable walking shoes were always a must.

Along the way, we enjoyed the variety of architecture, the diversity of the crowds, the beauty of the holiday window displays, the energy of the fur protesters and their horseback-riding police escorts, the aroma of Garrett's caramel popcorn, the steamy breath of the buggy horses, and the sounds of traffic cop whistles.

We each had our favorite stopping places: novelty and electronic shops for their playful gadgets, Stuart Brent's bookstore for its cozy ambiance, Niketown for its fun, Fourth Presbyterian church for its peace, and the Drake Hotel for its harp music. Sometimes we walked together and sometimes we separated, especially when the boys started bringing their girlfriends along. After meeting at Bloomingdale's piano at a designated time, we'd start our long hike back to the train.

Weaving hurriedly through the back streets (running late as usual), we'd pass by the piney scent of a Christmas tree lot, the open doors of old neighborhood churches, and the funky decor of a honky-tonk bar.

We have walked in freezing cold, balmy sunshine, staggering wind, drifting snow, mist, rain, and fog. We've been hot, cold, wet, tired, and cranky. We've traded baby bottles for carryout coffee, and two lovely daughters-in-law have joined our journey.

Making it back to the train station with minutes to spare, we'd settle in the top deck once again, thankful for the train's stuffy warmth and each other's shoulders to nap on.

Sadly, in a major corporate buyout in 2005, Marshall Field's became Macy's department store, and a host of similar traditions for thousands of other families changed. The decades-old custom of the Christmas windows went the same route. They have never been the same.

In the end, perhaps it doesn't matter, for it was really never about the windows. It was about the opportunity to share a good meal, talk of future dreams, hold hands, walk arm in arm, laugh, and love. Windows of time and togetherness. The best gifts of the season.

Partings Well Made

Embraces that speak volumes in their silence. Kisses and tears. Whispered words of parting. Finally, the agonizing moment of separation.

Security checkpoint, Midway Airport, Chicago. No ticketed passengers beyond this point. Because my son's arrival was delayed, I became a wandering voyeur, canvassing a sea of constantly changing faces and farewells.

Parents, college students, lovers, dear friends, and aging parents in wheelchairs all created farewell scenes that would far surpass any Hollywood dramatizations.

Before September 11, airport goodbyes consisted of curbside air kisses, as no-nonsense cops swept the traffic along. For those who took the time to journey with their loved ones to the gate, a light hug and a happy wave had to suffice, as passengers grabbed their carry-ons and hurried to their seats.

Post–September 11, the added security barriers at different checkpoints throughout the airport limit time and access with loved ones. Even in the relative calm of those few months following the terrorists' attack, the barriers were a constant reminder that things had changed, that the ordinary is sublime, and that when those we hold most dear are leaving us, these are not occasions to be taken lightly.

And indeed they are not.

I'm embarrassed to admit that I couldn't pull my eyes away from the farewells. The moments were too riveting, too poignant, and I found too much of my own heart being drawn in.

I knew that these were no casual airport goodbyes when I saw the parents of a college student hold each other and their son in a long three-way hug before letting him line up for the passengers-only security check. He was almost past the guard when his parents called him out of line and repeated the whole embrace again.

Trying not to stare at this scene, I looked to my left only to find a mother-daughter farewell. The daughter, sporting long, straight hair, a nose ring, shiny red shoes, and a backpack flung across her shoulder, was clasped closely to the chest of her conservatively dressed mother. After several long moments, the mother finally let go, held her daughter by the shoulders, and studied her face as she spoke softly to her. The daughter nodded patiently, as if she'd heard this speech before. And she probably had. But I knew the mother was only trying to prolong the moment, to memorize the youthful beauty of her child.

At last they parted, and as the daughter sauntered away, the mother stood watching with her arms crossed tightly over her chest, as if still trying to feel her daughter's presence.

I turned away from this sorrowful separation, only to be pulled into the romantic drama of two young lovers. He was loaded down with a huge pink-and-white-striped Victoria's Secret bag, which he dropped unceremoniously, pulling his girlfriend into a passionate kiss. This was followed by long hugs, soft cheek caresses, and more kisses.

With great difficulty, they finally broke apart. Leaving him at the security checkpoint, she turned away first and headed up the nearby escalator, her face contorted in anguish and tears.

Drawn into the suspense, I silently pleaded, *Oh, please smile. This is how he'll remember you.* As I watched, she looked away to find that she was almost to the top. Turning back, she broke into a brave smile, blew him a kiss, touched her heart, and then disappeared over the top of the landing and out of sight.

Her lover took a deep breath, discreetly wiped his eyes, and headed to the security line, the Victoria's Secret bag a lonely reminder of their parting passion.

Perhaps my most profound observation was that most people left behind at the security point did not leave immediately after their loved ones had departed for the gates. Instead, they stood like players unwilling to move offstage after their part was over. They watched as their loved ones strode away. They waited even when their loved ones were long out of sight. They wished, in longing body language, for the unlikely chance that their loved one might return for one more embrace.

Solitary statues left in a swirling sea of rushing departures.

There is a wonderful line in Shakespeare's *Julius Caesar* when Brutus and Cassius must go their separate ways and head off to battle and unknown futures. Brutus says:

Forever and forever, farewell, Cassius!
If we do meet again, why, we shall smile;
If not, why then this parting was well made.

Cassius repeats the farewell to Brutus.

Here in the sterility of an airport terminal, the most exquisitely beautiful "partings well made" were taking place over and over again.

I would have unabashedly continued my role as audience for these mesmerizing moments but, oh, joyful recognition, I spot a tall figure heading down the concourse toward me. It is my son, safely returning from his business trip. I have offered to pick him up just for the subtle gain of having a good one-on-one visit. Our eyes catch and we wave cheerfully.

As he crosses the line of security demarcation, we exchange warm greetings and a happy hug and kiss. Around us, glad tidings, laughter, and joyous words of welcome burst forth from other united families.

Heading toward the baggage claim area with my son, I take one last look around at my fellow actors, who are also exiting this human theater with loved ones by their sides.

Shakespeare would be pleased. Our smiles could light up a stage.

Moving Muriel

It's the screen porch she'll miss the most, and I don't blame her. Sitting in one of the porch's vintage, white wicker rocking chairs, one can watch the flutter of newly green crabapple leaves and smell the sweet perfume of the backyard lilacs wafting on the breeze.

Always flying, the American flag flaps gently from the porch's corner post. Spring birds call sweetly to each other. It is peaceful and calm—a perfect place to watch the comings and goings of the neighborhood and listen to the music of children's laughter as they play in each other's yards.

This is my mother-in-law's home of forty years. It is where her two older sons trekked home from college to visit and where her youngest son completed junior high and high school. It is the last home she shared with her husband of forty-eight years before being widowed. And although she has successfully lived alone and independently here for the past twenty years, it is now time to go.

At almost eighty-nine, Muriel has made her own decision to move to a retirement home, and we (her sons and daughters-in-law) are grateful. Some of the tasks that once seemed so simple to her are becoming a little harder: getting groceries, doing laundry, fixing dinner, driving. We worry about her falling, the quality of her meals, and her spending so much time alone.

Despite the fact that she is intellectually strong, an avid reader and skilled bridge player, it takes a lot of effort and responsibility to maintain a house. So when a lovely apartment at a nearby retirement community opened up this spring, she announced to our surprise that she was ready to move.

And in the blink of an eye, the house went up for sale.

It is a daunting task, both mentally and physically, to break up a home of forty years and decide what to do with a lifetime of possessions. Even though Muriel took her favorite things to her apartment and graciously allowed her sons, daughters-in-law, and grandchildren to take what they could use, there is much left behind.

And what do we do with it? My father-in-law's navy uniform from World War II? The trunk my husband's great-grandmother brought over from Germany? The myriad of family photos, travel souvenirs, newspaper clippings, and other paraphernalia that were treasures at the time?

Does it go to another family member's basement for another forty years, or do we get rid of it? There are a multitude of not-so-easy decisions to make. Who should make them? My husband and his brother take leading roles in this process, with my sister-in-law, myself, and nearby grandchildren filling in where needed. We are extremely grateful for each other's help.

And so I find myself sitting on the porch, enjoying the breeze and the smell of lilacs, and waiting for the auctioneer to come. This is one of my jobs.

Because my mother-in-law and father-in-law were avid and knowledgeable antique hunters, there are quite a few vintage items for the auctioneer to peruse: books, collectible glass and dishware, my father-in-law's clothes iron collection, lanterns, frames, brass candlesticks, milk bottles, and cabinets, to name just a few.

We can't help but wonder if there isn't some *Antique Road Show* treasure worth thousands in the mix. On the other hand, we feel a great need and desire to just get rid of the stuff. Who has the time, energy, and know-how to figure it all out?

We can only put our heads together, do our best, and count on the expertise of others. Hence, the auctioneer.

As I sit and wait for his arrival, I can only imagine what my mother-in-law must feel. We discussed the possibility of having our own garage sale for these things, but that presents an emotional challenge for all.

The items she and her husband collected were never as important as the garage sale and flea market experiences they shared: sunny Saturday morning browsings, the excitement of a find, learning and appreciating the history and craftsmanship of an item. No matter the value of a piece, how does one put a price on all those memories?

There are no easy answers. And so we decided to have the auctioneer haul off the leftovers rather than try to bargain away all of Muriel's happy collections ourselves.

Thankfully, by this stage we have already moved my mother-in-law into her new apartment, so she is spared this process. I don't find it so easy myself, and I don't even live here. I think about her walking out that door for the last time and my heart weeps.

It takes a lot of strength and courage to leave a home and neighborhood you love and adjust to a different environment and new faces, especially in the advanced years of life. I wonder if I could do it.

We already went through this physically and emotionally wrenching process two years ago, with my own widowed mother, moving her from Ohio to the same wonderful nearby retirement home where my mother-in-law has just settled. They are friends and both know other people there, so it is a good start.

It goes without saying, however, that there are a few pitfalls along the way in this life-altering process. Everything does not always run smoothly. Fatigue, impatience, and worry can create communication problems for all involved. Yet, efforts at peace, perseverance, and compassion ease the journey.

It is music to our ears, therefore, when we hear Muriel say, "I just love it here," and my own mother happily proclaim, "I think of this as home now." How grateful are we all for that?

Now when our mothers visit our homes and those of their grandchildren, they are thrilled to see their lovely things in use. And for us, their possessions are sweet daily reminders of their lifelong passions and personalities.

But the best gifts both mothers have given us in this moving process are not their earthly treasures, but their examples of dignity and grace under trying circumstances. They have made huge transitions with optimistic fortitude, moving forward in life's journey with poise, grateful for the new beginnings that are offered even in their late eighties.

For their children and grandchildren, this legacy is priceless.

Barn Wood Harvest

The barn is coming down and it is a beauty. It has sat on its foundation for well over a hundred years, its numerous coats of red paint faded and mellowed to the soft hue of a rooster.

For various reasons—structural, practical, and otherwise—the family reached the difficult conclusion that the barn was no longer serviceable. Not an easy choice, but not many are in a farmer's life.

This barn will die a slow, peaceful death, which is a good thing. Because some family members have decided to harvest its beautiful, worn, and weathered yellow pine boards for furniture, it is being dismantled one stubborn plank at a time.

And it's putting up a good fight. I should know. As a sissy city slicker, I have joined my daughter-in-law's family on this chilly March day to help harvest some wood.

It is Bernice's barn. She is my daughter-in-law's grandmother, and for all of her eighty years, she has lived on a farm. She knows the cycles of the natural world and this is one of them.

Always a cheerful and optimistic person, she is happy that some of the barn wood is being recycled to make a table and bench for my son and daughter-in-law's new home. But as I help with the labor, I think about the memories it must hold for her.

It is where her tall, ruggedly handsome husband, now deceased for twenty-eight years, milked the cows. It is where her

four children pitched in with the chores, assisted with the milking, and fed and watered the livestock. It is where she helped
out whenever needed, adding to her own farm responsibilities,
not the least of which was preparing a huge midday dinner for as
many as twelve farmhands, in addition to her own family, during
harvest time.

Positioned right across from the tidy, white farmhouse, the
cow barn was the nucleus of the farm's life—the orb around
which the day's work circled. It was the centerpiece of a
bucolic landscape.

Already my son and daughter-in-law have a beautiful hutch
made from the barn's cow stalls. It was a wedding gift from her
parents, and now these boards that we harvest today will form
the table that matches.

My husband and I have come to help. My son, daughter-in-
law, and her parents are already working when we arrive. We can
locate them by the pounding.

"Pound here," shouts a voice.

"Try this corner," answers another.

"Good job!" shouts a third, as the groan of a loosened board
cracks the silence.

"Hello!" we shout through the racket.

"Come on up!" they answer.

This is not as easy as it sounds. To make our entrance onto the
second floor hayloft, we must climb up a wobbly ladder that leans
through a hole in the second floor of the barn and then squeeze
under a makeshift railing that surrounds the opening.

Our coworkers stop their work momentarily to greet us,
and we are stunned by their appearance. All four smile out from
grime-coated faces, with wood chips in their hair and coats and
jeans smeared with dirt and dust.

What have we gotten ourselves into? In a few short moments,
my husband and I will look the same. We divide into pairs: one

person pounds upward from underneath the floor with a large log while the other uses a hammer to pry up the plank from above. These tasks look way too hard for me, so I happily volunteer to pound the nails out of the boards as they come free. Not having swung a hammer very often in my life (I prefer to wield a pen), I consider success to be hitting the nail and not my hand, as evidenced by the souvenir bruises I took home.

When the nails are out, I carry the fifteen- to eighteen-foot boards over to a growing pile and sweep off the dirt with a big push broom. Believe me, no workout in a gym can equal the physical labor on a farm. And our work is nothing compared with the daily labor of real farmers. I can feel all my muscles in action, and it isn't long before they start to protest. But with the others doing the grunt work, I can hardly sit down and take a breather.

Still, I pause between boards to watch the activity around me. It is obvious my daughter-in-law's mother grew up on this farm. Having helped her father with the milking years ago (and having inherited his bright blue eyes), she goes about the pounding and the pulling with a sense of easy strength and good cheer. She is home.

Clearly her daughter is of the same vein. This farm family raises strong and powerful women, and she is one of them. I recognize Grandmother Bernice's optimism in a third generation as I listen to my daughter-in-law's musical laughter echoing throughout the hayloft.

My husband, as usual, bursts with energy, tackling each ornery board with gusto and enthusiasm. He loves being outside and working with his hands. I think he missed his calling as a farmer.

My son and his father-in-law, the conservative and the liberal, work side by side in affable unity and humor. Despite their political differences, they always enjoy each other's company immensely. They epitomize constructive collaboration. Despite the occasional frustration and disappointment when a board snaps and is no longer usable, neither man places blame on the other. Patience and harmony rule the day.

Amid all the hustle and bustle, I am occasionally able to stop and catch my breath as I wait for the next board to come my way. An ethereal scene surrounds me. Decades of dust motes float up into the airy light of the rafters. The symmetry of the beams causes the barn to resemble the hull of an ancient ship. A spring snow drifts softly through the windows, showering the straw floor with frosty flakes and adding to the peaceful quiet. High up is the loft's open peak where the summer's hay harvest shot through its opening. Over in the corner rests the loft's door, a huge red puzzle piece waiting for placement.

Looking out the window to the barnyard, I admire the Black Angus cows whose gentle, brown eyes gaze back at me. Some gather under a shed's roof for protection from the snow. Others stand in defiance and let the flakes settle on their shiny black coats.

My daughter-in-law's uncle, the one who now farms this land, climbs the ladder and pokes his head through the floor opening to say hello and check out the action. He tells us that a pair of eagles has been circling over the nearby fields and several newborn calves are over in the side pen, if we want to take a look. Of course, we do.

Finally, having gathered enough boards for the project and having built up a serious hunger, we traipse across the road to a delicious meal that Bernice has been preparing.

I worry about our dust- and dirt-covered clothes, but Bernice does not. This is a working farm, she reminds us, and she's used to it. We simply take off our shoes, wash up, and settle down at the table, where the red barn forms a backdrop through her lovely lace-curtained windows.

This is a real midday farmer's meal: fork-tender beef roast, hot mashed potatoes and gravy, homemade coleslaw, warm buttermilk biscuits, and a steaming bowl of corn that is as sweet as the day it was picked on the farm.

Before we begin, however, we say the family's traditional grace. Bernice extends her strong, capable hands, and we form a circle around the bountiful table: "God is great, God is good, and we thank Him for His food. By His hand we all are fed; give us Lord our daily bread."

It is definitely a farmer's prayer. And one day soon, we will gather around my son and daughter-in-law's recycled barn-board table, admire its lovely grain burnished to a fine patina, and say that prayer once again. I will think of the long history of the cow barn, the day we shared in the spring snowstorm, and all the farm families that nurture the earth to feed the world.

For that, we give great thanks.

In Waiting

We are in a heightened state of waiting. Perched on the edge of two of life's great milestones, we anticipate the birth of our first grandchild and wrestle with the approaching loss of my husband's eighty-nine-year-old mother, Muriel. Both could happen at any time, perhaps even on the same day.

Although the book of Ecclesiastes says for everything there is a season, a time to be born and a time to die, it is difficult handling the two at the same time. Our emotions are on a seesaw: up one moment and down the next. We bounce between hope and sorrow, joy and sadness. Yet, despite these disparities, it is clearly a time for love.

When I visit my soon-to-be granddaughter's nursery, I see touches of love everywhere. Delightful gifts from family and friends sit in readiness. There are adorable hand-knit sweaters and booties, a row of little pink sleepers hanging neatly in the closet, a basketful of creative toys and stuffed animals, a bookcase filled with stimulating books, drawers of itsy-bitsy diapers, and an array of lotions and tonics for her every need.

Keeping watch over all is a lovely antique doll, a welcoming gift from her great-grandmother.

And when I visit my mother-in-law's apartment, I see signs of love everywhere as well: colorful flower arrangements and plants, cozy robes lined up in the closet, thoughtful gifts of books and music, a basket brimming with notes and cards filled with good wishes, plus lotions and supplies that resemble the baby's to meet her every need.

Keeping watch over all is her beautiful collection of antique dolls, carefully placed on the shelves of a vintage pine hutch where she can see them. They keep her company with happy memories. She has collected these dolls from antique shows and flea markets for over forty years, and they have given her much pleasure. She has meticulously named and catalogued each doll's history: the year it was made and by whom, the date and price of purchase, whether the clothes are original or not, the doll's materials, such as bisque, porcelain, or cloth. They have been her pride and joy and a great source of comfort and focus, especially after she was widowed twenty years ago.

She had never parted with a single doll until a few weeks ago. Having learned of her terminal illness around the first of November, my mother-in-law was bound and determined to make the most of the time left. And so when one daughter-in-law hosted a baby shower for my other daughter-in-law, Muriel set her sights on attending.

On a frosty sun-sparkled afternoon, she labored up a set of outdoor steps with the help of my sister-in-law, myself, and her walker in order to attend the party. She was clearly out of breath and fatigued from the effort. We settled her in a comfy chair where she could watch all the festivities and chat with family and friends. A short time later, when I asked how she was doing, she said, "Well, it has taken me about thirty minutes to regain my breath, but I'm here!"

There was great fun and laughter when my daughter-in-law unwrapped all her pretty gifts, but when she opened my mother-in-law's present, a burst of oohs and aahs filled the room. Out from careful wrappings came a tall, beautiful antique doll from my mother-in-law's collection.

We know from my sister-in-law who had helped her with the preparations that Muriel put great thought into selecting just the right doll for this first great-grandchild. We can only surmise how hard it must have been for her to break up the doll collection that had given her so much delight. She was accepting that her days were numbered. Yet, right from the time she learned of her diagnosis in the doctor's office, she had said, "Well, I've had a wonderful, healthy eighty-nine-years."

And so, in a gesture of grace, a charming vintage doll is passed from the end of a great-grandmother's long, well-lived life to the joyful beginning of her great-granddaughter's. Whether the two will meet on this earth or not, the doll symbolizes the unbroken bond of love that has already connected them.

In recent days, I have placed my hands into my mother-in-law's and sadly felt life ebbing from them. Yet, I have also shared in a miraculous moment when my daughter-in-law placed my hands on her rounded belly, and I felt the joyous roll and kick of new life from the baby within.

Both give me pause to ponder this amazing gift of life. One dearly loved person is exiting and one already dearly loved little person is soon to enter. As we wait in deepening sorrow for one and heightening anticipation for the other, we search for individual ways to express a tender goodbye and a welcoming hello.

My constant prayer is that God give them each a peaceful passage. May one go in serenity, and may the other enter safely and in good health. At this point, we can only trust and wait.

And although these events are at opposite ends of the great life cycle, we will rejoice as each occurs: one life's conclusion and one life's precious start.

Under our Christmas tree sits my mother-in-law's yellow wicker doll buggy that she pushed around the blocks of her home in Eldora, Iowa, more than eighty-five years ago. One day in the not-too-distant future, her great-granddaughter will perhaps pursue the same pleasure, happily (and very carefully) pushing her great-grandmother's vintage doll around her own block. The life cycle continues. As the book of Ecclesiastes concludes, there is a time to mourn and a time to dance. And although we may weep awhile both in mourning and in joy, in honor of both lives, we will also surely dance. And in doing so, we will remember that "He has made everything beautiful in its time."

～

DECEMBER 17, 2006
Muriel Louise Mamminga, lovingly mourned

DECEMBER 22, 2006
Lily Clara Mamminga, joyously welcomed

Becoming a Grandmother

She smiled at me. She was only a couple of hours old, but she smiled at me. I know this because I am her grandmother.

The experts, of course, say that babies don't smile until they are at least a month old, but what do the experts know? They attribute any earlier smiling to gas or reflexive action or any number of physical quirks. But they are wrong.

She smiles at me every time I hold her. This is the truth. And if you don't believe me, you can ask Grandpa. She smiles at him, too. She also smiles at her other grandma and grandpa, so there you have it. A full-fledged 100 percent-accurate scientific poll.

It is wonderful entering the world of grandparenthood. When our son sent a text message to us four new grandparents in the hospital waiting room (ah, the world of electronics!) announcing that our granddaughter had been born, my husband and I hugged each other with a newfound amazement.

How had we gone from teenage sweethearts to parents to grandparents so swiftly? But, oh, what a sweet milestone to share together. We looked at each other in disbelief. Grandpa and grandma? Awesome!

I have been listening to our friends go on and on about their grandchildren for years. Now, they are about to get payback in a gargantuan grandma way.

You want pictures? I got 'em. You want descriptions? Let me count the ways. You want me to change the subject? Not going to happen.

I am a goo-goo ga-ga grandma, and there's no stopping me now.

One of the first delightful choices we grandparents had to make was what names we would like to be called. Even though our granddaughter won't start speaking for about a year (though, as we already know, the experts can be wrong), we have to set the groundwork early. After all, this name thing is a monumental decision—one that will last a lifetime.

I've decided on Nana because that is what my son called me as a toddler before he could pronounce Mama. I always found it endearing and hope my granddaughter will, too. One grandfather wants to be called Papa, and because the four of us are of a certain generation, we've joked about becoming the Nanas and the Papas. We certainly ooh and coo harmoniously together whenever we are around our grandbaby, but two of us grandparents are opting for the tried and true Grandma and Grandpa, saving her from one of what are sure to be many embarrassing grandparent moments.

At least, those are the names we've chosen for ourselves. Our granddaughter may have other ideas. We might be Moomoo or Poopoo for all we know. We'll let her decide. All four of us have surmised, however, that at four weeks old she's already recognized us as *meshuga mishpacha*, the Hebrew words for "crazy family."

As the Bears scrambled down a snowy field in search of a Super Bowl play-off slot, most adults in all Chicagoland were glued to the television. But as the game played in the background, we four grandparents were glued to the real star: our granddaughter. Talking baby talk to her from behind the couch as her mother held her, we oohed and cooed and generally made babbling fools of ourselves.

She stared at us in wide-eyed wonder, moving her bright eyes from one goofy grandparent to the other. As she kicked the little blue-and-orange Bear booties that her daddy had placed over her tiny pink outfit, she looked up at the four of us with a puzzled expression that seemed to say, "What have I gotten myself into?"

Each one of us four grandparents has commented to another that we cannot believe such a tiny baby can be so fascinating. Who would have guessed that we can be entertained for hours just holding and staring at her—her long slender fingers, the intricate shape of her ears, her tiny mouth, and her expressive eyebrows. When she yawns or stretches, you'd think it was the Fourth of July by our amazed expressions.

There is a limit to our expertise, however. Even we have to admit that when she gets fussy or starts to cry or has a poopy diaper, only her parents have the right touch. And back she goes.

But the best part of becoming grandparents is the anticipation of being able to play with a child again. Even when our son called to say our daughter-in-law was in labor and the baby was expected to be born in a couple of hours, my husband and I felt an urgent need to put the dolls from her great-grandmother in order before she was born.

"Hurry!" I shouted to my husband, as if she was coming to play any minute. "We've got to get the dolls ready!"

And so we did. The two of us scrambled around in a panic, placing the dolls neatly in a cabinet where she could reach them if she were a toddler. Satisfied, we drove off to the hospital to await her birth.

Not only are the dolls ready, but Grandpa has a new set of blocks waiting in the wings and Nana has teacups and saucers, and out in the garage is a vintage scooter that we found at the flea market. Of course, at four weeks old, it will be awhile before she can use them. (If, by chance, you stop by and see Grandpa building a tower with his blocks or Nana having tea at a tiny table with miniature cups and saucers, know that we are just practicing.)

One of the most profound and daunting aspects of becoming a grandparent is this newfound sense of the future. Before our granddaughter's birth, the future seemed a vague and distant thing. But now, two generations removed from us, she makes the future seem much more tangible and real.

And with this realization comes a whole new sense of responsibility, not only for her well-being but also for the world she'll live in. Issues such as world peace, the environment, relationships, faith, and learning opportunities, which were always important, suddenly take on a more intimate meaning. More than ever before, we want the wars to end, the glaciers to stop melting, the religious faiths to respect each other, and the smog to clear so that the stars can shine, not only for her future but for the future of all the little grandchildren of the world.

Perhaps becoming a grandparent is God's way of giving us one last nudge to make the world a better place before we leave it. And what could make that nudge more convincing than knowing the footsteps that follow yours are your grandchild's?

Just the other day, I held my granddaughter on my chest for over an hour. She snuggled dreamily against me in a cozy nap. Resting her head on my shoulder, she tucked her little hand under her chin and curled her tiny knees up under her bottom. I could feel her small heart beating against mine, the two hearts together like a valentine of love.

I'm sure she was smiling, and so was I.

Learning Curves

I am always ready to learn, although I do not always like being taught.

—WINSTON CHURCHILL

Rip Van Winkle Returns to School

It was a long maternity leave. Twenty years, in fact, since I walked out of my third-floor classroom with its view of the river, waved goodbye to my cheerful class of seventh-graders, and at seven months pregnant went home to await the birth of my first child.

Three sons later, at the age of forty-eight, with a résumé that included Cub Scout leader, Sunday school teacher, room mother, and freelance writer, I walked back in.

Hired at the last minute by my former school district as the fifth high school journalism/English instructor they'd been through in five years (they were desperate), I had just ten days to read the *Odyssey*, acclimate myself to block scheduling, and figure out new high-tech procedures, such as using a Dynacom system. Where to begin?

My instincts ruled. I needed a makeover.

As luck would have it, the beauty counter consultant was a recent high school grad.

"What tips can you give me?" I implored the eighteen-year-old as she swathed my eyelids with plum-berry shadow.

Stepping back to assess my face, she pondered the question with Einstein-like seriousness. "Just remember one thing," she said as she moved in to adjust her purplish palette. "They don't want to be there."

With this nugget of advice, plum-berry-shadowed eyes, and CliffsNotes for the *Odyssey* stuck in my briefcase, I strode back into the hallways of academia.

Like Rip Van Winkle of yore, I was in for a rude awakening. Things had changed.

First off, simple daily procedures like taking attendance and providing discipline had gone high tech. Back in the 1970s, we wrote absent kids' names on a piece of scrap paper and stuck it on a nail outside the door. If a kid misbehaved, we simply invited him in for a little chat during after-school detention.

Flash forward to the 1990s. I found myself scrambling to find the required No. 2 pencil to fill in little bubbles for the right day and week on a Scantron sheet next to absent students' names, and then re-recording absentees in a separate record book.

Misbehavior and truancy resulted in complicated paperwork involving a scaled system of consequences, parent notifications, loss of privileges, and zero hour detentions (i.e., before school). I needed a personal secretary to keep it all straight.

Twenty years ago, Gertrude, the no-nonsense school secretary, shouted announcements into a raspy PA system. The 1990s version showcased student Jay Leno wannabes on each individual classroom's thirty-inch TV screen, rendering creative readings of the week's activities. I'm not sure which method is better. Either way, the kids don't listen. Gossip from their friends is much more newsworthy.

Instruction time was another shocker. I discovered classroom periods had changed from forty-two-minute sprints to ninety-minute marathons. The first had been short and to the point; the second was multi-activity driven. Both had their pros and cons. Despite the differences in instructional time, I found students still struggling with parts of speech.

What had not changed was the bathroom dashes between classes. Students and teachers are still in the same boat on this one. You know someone has to go when you see him or her weaving wildly down crowded halls with a glazed but determined look on his or her face. That person was often me. It took most of a semester, but I finally got my plumbing to coincide with the five-minute passing schedule. Don't even think about ringing a bell as a joke.

Perhaps the most drastic and unsettling change I observed was the need for tighter security and safety. Twenty years ago, the school's atmosphere was open, friendly, fun. Now it is tight, suspicious, serious. Teachers wear identification badges, receive latex gloves and warnings about blood-borne pathogens, and learn the protocol for handling strangers who enter the building and emergency procedures for locking our doors. A policeman (ironically, a former seventh-grade student of mine) patrols the halls.

"I thought I came here to teach, not run security," I sometimes mumbled to myself while standing at my appointed guard station between classes.

I am frequently asked if students have changed much in twenty years. That's a hard one. Problems at home seem more prevalent, or at least they're discussed more openly. Swearing is common in the hallways, and a myriad of students appear extremely tired, many of them working after-school jobs with late hours.

I experienced a few upsetting incidents when a kid lost it and became an aggressive bully. It took all I could muster intellectually and physically to hold those situations together. But there were a few moments when I went over the edge as well. One day I lost my cool over comma rules, of all things. Patience went out the window. As it often did for some of the students, fatigue and frustration had gotten the best of me.

My most gratifying discovery was that high school students continually defy their negative stereotypes. I found them sensitive, articulate, and playful. Despite the existence of cliques, I observed many instances of students including someone who was left out or voluntarily helping someone struggling with an assignment. On a daily basis, I witnessed gentle acts of kindness, riveting gestures of loyalty, and comic punch lines that would put the whole cast of *Saturday Night Live* to shame.

Just like Old Rip, I was a little dazed and confused upon re-entry, but, unlike Rip, I didn't have the luxury of sitting around. There was too much to learn. By the time the last school bell rang at the end of the year, I'd made the transition.

"You taught us good," wrote one student before heading out the doors to summer's freedom.

Now, about those parts of speech.

Technology Aversion

I am unplugged and I like it that way.

Do not call me on my cell phone. It's never on.

Email me only if you're in no hurry for a response.

Forget telling me to go online. It's like sending me to Siberia.

And frankly, I just don't want to go there.

I'm a techno dropout and I hope to stay that way. It's not that I couldn't learn to use all that technology out there, I just choose not to try.

This is heresy for those who always carry their cell phones, people who are bonded to their email accounts like spiders to their webs and surf the internet for the latest news flash all the livelong day.

I'll take a pass, thank you very much.

Although most people seem to feel this technology is a convenience, I believe just the opposite. Too much time, too much trouble. Cell phones need recharging, emails need returning, and computers need repairing. For me, depending on these gadgets can turn my day into a maze of madness.

Being disconnected does have its disadvantages, however. Watching all those people walking and driving around with cell phones makes me feel friendless. I thought I had a social life, but I guess not.

Not using email can also keep me out of the loop. Yet emails can eat up my day faster than a woodpecker on a rotten tree. So, to all those sentimental stories, sex ads, jokes, scams, and spams, I say, "No thank you, ma'am."

I admit, computers are necessary for many kinds of work, including my own. But when computers go awry, as mine often seems to do, it can just about drive me over the edge. Out of the blue (as at this very moment!), it will start to make a strange humming noise and, more often than not, freeze up as dead as Marley's ghost. Suddenly I resemble a frantic character in a 1920s silent movie running around mouthing screams of *Help! Save me!*

Alas, there is no rescuer in sight, and I must do what I am loath to do. I dial the mysterious help line. Here I am greeted by a customer service associate on the other side of the earth who walks me through backward-slash, forward-slash maneuvers as if we're learning the intricate steps of a tango. Before long, I am on my hands and knees crawling under my desk and around the room as I unplug and replug a series of tangled cords, I know not why.

Fortunately, after about two hours of these puzzling field exercises, the customer service associate not only has my computer back up and running, but is my new best friend and hero.

Nevertheless, I hope not to have to call him anytime soon.

Friends and family have enthusiastically espoused the digital world and tried to connect me, but I just yawn and look the other way.

"Send me an attachment," my son says.

"I don't do attachments," I answer.

"You'd love an iPod because you can create your own tune list," a friend advises.

"I'd rather hum," I say.

"Go online to this website and download the information," suggests my sister.

"Can't you just tell me about it?" I ask.

Add to my list that I rarely watch TV or go to movies, and you can just about hear a pin drop out there in my corner of cyberspace. My family has tried to nudge me along in the world of technology by giving me a cell phone. Yet on our annual Thanksgiving trip to Chicago, when we decided to split up for an hour and regroup, I was a dismal failure.

"Everyone got their cell phones on?" asked one son. "Mom?"

"I didn't bring mine," I sheepishly replied. "I unloaded it to make my purse lighter."

Sighs all around.

They also gave me a digital camera for Christmas, yet the first time I went to the store to print the photos, the store's computer crashed and my hour's worth of work was gone.

"What happened?" I asked.

"Don't know," the clerk said with a shrug.

See what I mean?!

I am delighted when I discover others who share my aversion to high-tech stuff. Recently, a doctor told me he prefers to jot his notes on sticky pads than to scribble them on a Palm Pilot. It's easier and faster. You the man, Doc.

A college professor I know refuses to own a cell phone. He'd rather discuss the details of the Ottoman Empire in person with his students. It's no wonder he's a Cambridge scholar.

And my lifelong friend from kindergarten says don't even bother to email her. She'd rather hear my voice. Amen, sister.

Yet, being a technological holdout is becoming more and more difficult. Refusing to participate is like swimming against the strong current of progress. Often, I feel how the last of the horseback riders must have felt at the turn of the twentieth century as those newfangled cars whizzed by, scaring the daylights out of horses and riders. (Just think of the problems we would have avoided if we'd kept to horses!)

To be fair, I do use and need a small amount of this technology. And I acknowledge that much of it is extremely convenient and helpful to many people's lives, families, and businesses.

But it can also be a trap that fills one's day with obligations. Not being drawn into that black hole provides a satisfying sense of freedom.

So, give me an old-fashioned wall calendar to pencil in my appointments, a pad of paper for my notes, a newspaper for news, a book for entertainment, and the sound of the birds for music, and I'm a happy camper.

"But how will you get by without using technology?" friends ask in disbelief.

In the simplest possible way, I intend to find out.

Washed-Up Dishwasher

I'm giving up my dishwasher. That cranky, noisy, unreliable machine is out the door. Our current apparatus is well over ten years old and although it still runs, it does a lousy job. It's time to either buy a new one or give it up. And since my New Year's resolution is to take greener steps for our environmentally troubled earth, my dishwasher could be the first appliance to go.

Because there is conflicting research out there about whether using a dishwasher or washing by hand is more environmentally friendly, I decide to check in with a dishwashing expert: my husband. For all thirty-seven years of our marriage, this gem of a guy has done the majority of our dinner dishes. Scrubbing the pots and pans and loading the dishwasher have been his tasks. I cook and he cleans up.

This includes all the meals while our three hungry boys were growing up, birthday parties, Thanksgiving dinners for twenty-seven years in a row, and a huge variety of other gatherings with friends and family.

Even he admits that he has had it with the dishwasher. By the time he's done all the scraping and rinsing, the dishes look clean enough to go back on the shelves. Instead, they are loaded into that endlessly droning contraption that sounds like a dinosaur munching gravel for hours on end.

Granted, there is the satisfaction of hiding the dirty dishes in the dishwasher in order to have an instantly clean counter, but the tedious task of unloading and putting away (my job) negates that benefit in the snap of a soap bubble.

Proponents of environmentally friendly dishwashers say the machines are all right as long as you eliminate scraping and rinsing and turn off the dry feature. Now who does that?

In addition to the energy required to manufacture and then to run them, the machines reportedly use between seven and fifteen gallons of water per cycle. Hand-washing proponents will tell you they don't come close to using that much water, even though some dishwashing machine research suggests otherwise. (Hmm, I wonder who wrote those reports?)

At our house there are only the two of us now, and on our test drive without the dishwasher for the past several weeks, we have discovered some pleasant surprises.

First of all, the dinner dishes get done a lot faster without all that loading and unloading. My husband still washes, but I dry and put them away. It's a great time to continue our dinnertime conversation.

We also no longer hunt for that utensil that has been in the dishwasher for three days, waiting for a full load to run. It's already back in its drawer.

Recently, we entertained sixteen longtime friends for dinner, and even the dishwashing became a part of the evening's entertainment. When the ladies insisted on helping with the dishes, my husband graciously accepted and bowed out. We had a blast visiting and laughing in the kitchen as I washed and they dried and put away. The counters were empty by the time everyone headed out the door after midnight.

Now, that's a nice way to end a party.

There's something comforting about washing dishes in warm, soapy water, and it also provides a great time to think and reflect.

I'm often reminded of my growing-up years when my sister and I were required to wash and dry the dinner dishes for our family of seven. We thought this a great injustice, so to counter our complaining, our mother insisted that we sing through our repertoire of Girl Scouts songs.

You never heard a more dismal display of melodies in your life. "I'm Happy When I'm Hiking" sounded like a funeral dirge. Our soulless singing eventually made even our grumpy selves start to laugh. We not only got the dishes done, but in the process added a treasured memory to our collection.

When my sons were young, they learned about dishwashing at our family's log cabin in Wisconsin. For over half a century, the dishes have been washed in a large, round enamel pan. Despite the number of dirty dishes, someone gladly volunteers to wash and another to dry. It's almost like a competition for who gets to do it. From the happy chatter that echoes out of that tiny kitchen, you would think it was fun instead of work.

And actually, it is.

Opportunities to visit, reflect, and help others are all part of the dishwashing game. Obviously, giving up the dishwasher is not for everyone. But for me, it is.

And, happily, I've got a song to sing.

Cubby Bear Bliss

I know next to nothing about baseball, but that doesn't stop me from being a die-hard Cubs fan. Just buy me some peanuts and Cracker Jack and, as the song says, I don't care if I ever get back.

As the "Lovable Losers" run the bases into what appears to be another dismal season, I can't wait to head out to the ballpark. Wrigley Field tops my summer to-do list.

I won't know who's playing until I remember to ask on the way to the game. It's doubtful I can name a single player. Okay, maybe. Is Kerry Wood still on the roster? I do know the manager is Dusty Baker. Oh wait, that was a season or two ago. And that Sammy Sosa just hit his 600th home run for, oh, I mean against the Cubs.

I also know the Cubs' catcher got tossed for swinging at his own player instead of the ball and that the sacred ivy wall has ads on its outfield doors, which in my view is a travesty. And that's about it.

Nevertheless, donning my blue Cubby Bear hat and a red shirt is one of my finest fashionista moments. Luckily, I get to do this two or three times a year.

Given my lack of statistical knowledge, some might say I am not a true fan. But that is like saying there's no backside to the moon just because you can't see it. Of course I am a Cubs fan! Wouldn't a fan go to years of Cubs conventions and stand in line for hours to get what's-his-name's autograph for her kids? And wouldn't a true fan give up lollygagging on the white sands of a Maui beach to haul those same kids out to Mesa, Arizona, for Cubs spring training? And wouldn't a true blue fan interview the awesome gentleman Ron Santo (who even *I* know should be in the Hall of Fame) and chat with Harry Caray, given the chance? Been there, done that. I rest my case.

So, if I'm not paying attention to the logistics of the game, how the heck can I love it? Let me count the ways.

First is my version of the pregame show: driving Lake Shore Drive, no matter how heavy the traffic, so I can see Buckingham Fountain, Lake Michigan, and the sailboats; finding a street parking spot, which is like squeezing our car into a shoe two sizes too small; and walking along quiet streets lined with charming gardens and burly brownstones and wondering why the heck I didn't live here in my youth like the savvy young folks of today.

Like a switch hitter, the atmosphere changes gear as we near the park with the crowds exiting the L, the barking ticket scalpers, and the boisterous bar browsers. Purchasing bags of peanuts from a street vendor, we head to the Harry Caray statue and tap our toes to the lively Cubby combo as we wait to meet family or friends.

The game hasn't even started and I'm having a ball.

Heading into the park early, as true Cubs fans do, of course, we take time to scope out the easy-going batting practice where each crack of the bat reminds us of past Cubs dreams come true. Greeting the friendly ushers (could there be a better job?), we head to our seats climbing steep steps and winding up ramps that make me feel like I'm in a Salvador Dali painting.

And it's a must to stop and enjoy the view of the city skyline stretching out to the lakefront, with its ancient church steeples rising up like flowers in a field. Grabbing some hot dogs, we finally settle into our seats.

In our high perches, we're in baseball heaven as we munch on our lunch and watch the field crew sweep, chalk, tap, and sprinkle the playing field. The excitement mounts. The organ plays. Men remove their hats. "The Star-Spangled Banner" surges forth. And in humbling awe, thirty-nine thousand fans grant the stadium silence for a moment of honor.

Play ball!

As the game begins, there's no better time to people-watch. Babies and babes, old folks and handsome hipsters, young kids and whole families are all talking and smiling and watching the game and filling out score cards and eating and drinking and having a delightful time, no matter what the score.

Because it's never about the game.

It's always about being with my family, sitting side by side, laughing, visiting, relishing the lake breeze, the blue bowl of the sky, the wispy white clouds, the flapping flags, and the diverse mix of voices raised in gleeful song for the seventh-inning stretch. And yes, despite all the cheering, yelling, clapping, and booing, and whatever the final score, a contented, happy peace surrounds me.

It all adds up to a win. A true fan has spoken. Now pass me the peanuts. I see Ryne Sandberg's flag flying. He must be up to bat.

Sailing Away

I broke the law.

Of course, I did not do it on purpose. But as any law officer will attest, ignorance of the law is no excuse.

I was not speeding. I was not illegally parked. I did not run a toll. I was simply sailing. Sailing? Who gets a ticket while sailing? As luck would have it, I do.

As the old song goes, "I was sailing along on Moonlight Bay." Well, not exactly.

It was a beautiful afternoon on the Fourth of July in northern Wisconsin as I awaited my family's arrival at our cabin. All was ready for our expected crew of twelve: fishing boat in the water, food in the fridge, beds made.

"Why don't you relax and go for a sail?" my husband suggested. (See, it is really his fault.)

I hadn't been sailing yet that summer. Gazing out at the blue lake and a blowing wind, I thought, *Why not?*

My sailboat is small, perfect for one or an occasional passenger perched near the bow. I have been a sailor since I was twelve years old, and few things give me more pleasure than heading out onto the water in my little boat to test my wits against the wind. There is only the soft sound of water rushing against the hull and the beautiful backdrop of the forested lake offering peaceful solitude. Unless, of course, you're about to be stopped by a warden.

I had just accomplished a hard tack against the wind to get out of our bay and into more open water when I noticed a powerful fishing boat approaching at a slow speed. Sometimes other sailors on the lake will approach to compare sailing notes. So I offered a friendly wave and a smile.

The man at the wheel waved back. It seemed odd that he was tailing me so closely, but I assumed that he was interested in my boat.

He was. And as the boat pulled up, I realized that he was a she: a steely, short-haired woman packing a pistol and wearing a bulletproof vest. I was in trouble.

"Hello!" she shouted over the wind.

"Hello!" I shouted back, wondering what was up.

"Do you have a valid sailboat registration with you?" she asked.

"No," I answered honestly. "Sailboats don't need registrations, only motorized boats do."

"Sailboats do if they are over twelve feet," she replied.

"Mine's not over twelve feet," I countered.

"It says fourteen hundred right on the side" she answered.

"That must be the model number," I blustered.

"No, it means you have a fourteen-foot boat, so I'll need to write you a citation."

"Can't you just give me a warning?" I pleaded.

"No," she answered. "I must be consistent."

Even though I was in moving water, I knew I was stuck. "How much is the ticket?" I asked, bracing myself.

"One hundred and eighty-six dollars," she replied.

I just about toppled out of my boat. One hundred and eighty-six dollars! Was she kidding?! I looked at her pistol and decided probably not.

During this whole conversation, I was struggling to control my sail against a blowing breeze by heading into the wind and letting my sail go slack. It's not exactly like stepping on the brakes or pulling the car over to the side of the road. But apparently, a sailor's wind was not a warden's worry.

With about thirty feet of water between us, she shouted out her questions: Name? Address? Age? I miserably shouted my answers back, ducking the wildly flapping boom like a middle-aged woman practicing hip-hop out in the middle of the lake.

For a moment, I thought about pretending my boat was out of control and just sailing away, but I figured she'd tailgate me until I ran aground. I also thought about capsizing as a diversion, but I sensed she'd probably hand me the ticket while I was treading water next to my half-submerged boat.

Thankfully, common sense prevailed, for I'd heard of this warden's reputation. Newspaper accounts reported that she had once hidden in the woods for over forty-eight hours in an effort to entrap out-of-season hunters. You didn't mess with this badge number.

Finally, she cruised up on my port side, handing me the ticket and actually pointing a finger at the boating regulations book for me to read as proof.

As luck would have it, my sailing ropes wrapped around her boat cleats, tangling our vessels up tighter than a fish on a barbed hook. Capsizing the warden would have been the last thing I needed.

At last I was set free (both literally and figuratively) and with my ticket tucked in the bottom of my swimsuit (an appropriate place if there ever was one), I cruised home, the wind, as they say, out of my sails. My husband and I immediately measured my boat upon return: thirteen feet, eight inches. Guilty as charged.

Several weeks later, to my further chagrin, an embarrassing newspaper account appeared. There's misery in company, however, and over half the newspaper page was devoted to Department of Natural Resources violations, with a great many offenders coming from Illinois. It seems we Illinoisans keep the Wisconsin tills full, not only with our tourism but also with our negligence.

But I felt better when I read about the guy who got a $148.20 fine for failing to cover a battery in a boat; the fisherman who was nailed $248.60 for keeping a 13½-inch bass (apparently a smidge too short); and the dude who got socked for $160.80 for "overloading a pontoon with eighteen people—only two of whom were under a hundred pounds." Was there a scale? And how exactly did the powers that be arrive at those odd dollar and cents amounts?

Obviously, the laws exist for the protection of the lakes, the wildlife, and the people. And those big fines will make most of us pay much closer attention. My check's in the mail and the registration is ordered. Mea culpa.

But as I scanned the columns for my crime, a lucky surprise greeted me. My tricky last name was botched beyond recognition. Thank you, Sister Wind!

At least, that's my story and I'm sticking to it.

Leap of Faith

They dream big. Rock star, business owner, international marketing director. Eighteen-year-old seniors on the cusp of their graduation look down the river of their dreams and see wide open spaces with endless possibilities.

As their teacher, I like it. I like their verve, attitude, and confidence. I want some for myself.

Sitting in the cool, gray high school cafeteria these last few days of school, I listened to my seniors in advanced speech class as they shared their goals and dreams in front of their peers.

I am amazed by their visions of success. Self-doubt does not exist. They speak with sparkling eyes and enthusiastic voices that lend instant credibility to their goals, no matter how lofty or obscure.

When Peter says he can hear musical compositions in his head and wants to be a rock star, no one laughs. We'll be the first in line to buy his CDs. When Brittany says she wants to be a sports anchorwoman, we know we'll tune in. When Kevin says he wants to direct films, we envision his name on the credits.

I ponder these youthful outlooks as I pack up my classroom for the last time, not for the summer but for good. I have decided to leave teaching.

My twelve-year career in education began in the early 1970s at a junior high school, when I was fresh out of college and pursuing my own dream as an English teacher. It stopped six years later when I started my family and resumed twenty years after that. In between, I raised my three sons and worked as a freelance writer. Ten days before school started in the fall of 1997, nursing a need for change, I answered the call for a high school journalism teacher.

But on a cold day this past January, as I stood alone in my classroom, the idea slid slowly but perceptively into my head: perhaps it was time to make a course change and move on. My reasons are varied and complex, but mainly I want to get back to my own writing and see where it leads. If there is anything I've learned from teenagers these last six years, it's that the shackles of fear and failure do not hold them down. And so with a big breath, I run off the end of the dock and take a flying leap, not sure of where I'll land.

There are things I won't miss about teaching: the apathy and indifference of some students, the endless after-school work to read and grade, the challenging students that tested my patience and temper.

But there are so many more things that I will miss: amazing creativity, belly-shaking laughter, and some of the finest, most dedicated colleagues one could hope to work with over a lifetime.

On the last day of school, I took my advanced speech class down to the river to provide a picturesque setting for their farewell speeches. Although they couldn't wait to graduate and get out of town, I wanted to place them in the midst of their hometown to say their goodbyes.

As we sat in the shade of the river walk pavilion, the early morning sunlight sparkled off the river and bounced up to the pavilion's pitched, cobwebbed ceiling. Behind us, the historic Challenge Windmills spun in lazy circles, casting symmetrical shadows across meandering paths.

One by one, each student strode confidently to the apex of the eight-point star in the pavilion's center to say farewell. As we listened intently to their funny high school stories and plans for the summer, the sweet song of water rushing over a nearby dam whispered that freedom was just around the bend.

I knew that I was experiencing the epitome of teaching: when all is going well, when laughter, camaraderie, and ideas fill the air, when clear-eyed youths look down a river of hope and see a bright light beckoning.

For me, it was a perfect way to end a teaching career. And with that youthful energy embedded in my soul like a sparkling prism, it was a perfect way to step into my own flowing river of hopes and dreams and begin again.

Child-Rearing Changes

Thankfully, the babies haven't changed. But the rules for caring for them have, and that spells trouble for new grandparents.

When our daughter-in-law was rushed to the hospital for an emergency appendectomy, Grandpa and I were called on to care for our four-week-old granddaughter. Racing to the emergency room to retrieve her, we were confident that the wisdom and experience of raising our own three sons would guide us through the next two nights and two days with her.

We quickly discovered, however, we were once again nursery novices.

Our first hurdle was the car seat. Locking her bucket in place was no problem. Getting it out was. Even at four weeks old, our little granddaughter knew something was up as she watched Grandpa wrestle to unlock her from the car.

"You just push this red button in the back," our son had advised. But in the dark of night, where the heck was the button and why wouldn't it unlock?

Other grandparent friends have struggled with this same issue and admitted to just about pulling out the whole back seat to get the dang car seat out. In fact, thirty years ago when our first son was born, we didn't even have car seats. Our friends confessed that they put their toddlers in the back end of the station wagon and let them crawl around. Clearly, those were very different times, before the introduction of safety regulations or safety devices to guide us.

Our next challenge was thawing out the frozen breast milk in order to feed the now hungry baby. Thankfully, our other daughter-in-law, who is mother to our five-month-old granddaughter, became our mommy consultant.

No microwaving (it breaks down the enzymes). No placing in boiling water. Just gentle, warm water thawing.

This was all fine, except at my first 1:30 a.m. feeding, by the time I got my granddaughter's diaper changed and the bottle warmed, she had gone back to sleep.

There are also new methods for putting babies to bed. Back in our Dark Ages, we were instructed to put the babies on their tummies and cover them with warm blankets. Nowadays, this is a big no-no. Babies are to be placed on their backs with no loose blankets. Consequently, this has dramatically reduced the incidence of Sudden Infant Death Syndrome.

As I slept (and I use that word loosely) on the couch next to my granddaughter's bassinet, I checked on her all through the night to see if she was warm enough. When she peeped or sighed, I checked to see if she was hungry. When she was quiet, I checked to see if she was still breathing. Nana resembled the Energizer Bunny.

She, of course, slept like a baby and that's all that mattered.

By Day Two, I knew she needed a bath, but the baby tub was some new-fangled contraption that fit over the kitchen sink with a sling strung in the middle. Who knew which end was up? Back in our day, we just used the kitchen sink, holding the baby in the crook of an arm as we soaped and splashed. Baby and mother were usually both soaked by the end, but it worked.

The mystery tub was too much of a challenge after a sleepless night, so I opted for a sponge bath and nixed the task of shampooing her fine, dark hair. To my sleepy eyes, she still looked presentable.

Of course, a myriad of other things have changed since our early days as parents. Crib slats are required to be much closer together to prevent little heads from getting stuck. (You might as well throw away those old cribs you've been saving all these years.) Strollers resemble a complete jungle gym and, together with the car seat, weigh enough to stress even the buffest mom or dad. Bottles are completely aerodynamic, as long as you can figure out how to screw the nipple on. Doctors recommend that solid foods be presented at a much later age and that they come from an organic source. I don't think my granddaughter's first sentence will resemble my son's at eighteen months: "John wants more Coke!"

Thankfully, burping and diapering are pretty much the same, provided you can figure out the front of the diaper and how to unstick the tabs. Grandpa had not changed a diaper in twenty-three years and, as luck would have it, he was treated to a very poopy one. But he managed to get the job done.

Fortunately, my daughter-in-law's surgery went well, and when our son brought her home from the hospital, they walked in to see their beautiful baby snuggled on her grandpa's warm shoulder. Both were dozing.

There was a little poop stain on the back of her pretty sleeper, the result of Grandpa's changing technique, and her hair looked a bit greasy, I admit. But she was clean and dry and burped and fed. Most importantly, she'd been held, read to, and even sung to in Nana's off-key voice.

Despite all the changes in child-rearing, there is one thing we outdated grandparents are very good at. And that is providing our steadfast love.

Never changes. Never ends.

Owner's Manual

It was a dark and stormy night. Or at least in my nightmares it seems that way. Actually, it was a bright and sunny day when our tire blew out. If it had been a dark and stormy night, we would really have been in trouble.

It was difficult enough trying to figure out how to assemble the jack, locate the spare, and find the axle in broad daylight. Current car commercials make one think that the technical engineering of our automobiles would put them right up there with the Mars spacecraft. Alas, somewhere along this high-tech pursuit, someone forgot about keeping the jack and spare tire instructions simple. After our recent experience, I'd put changing a tire right up there with solving a Rubik's Cube.

Setting off on a twenty-mile trip to town from our cabin on a beautiful fall day in northern Wisconsin, my husband and I heard a weird noise coming from the right side of our car, as if we were dragging a big stick. For once in our lives, we decided not to ignore a car sound we could not identify and stopped to take a look.

To our surprise, the back right tire was flatter than a run-over penny on a train track. Turning the car around, we slowly drove the half mile back to the cabin where we would be able to change the tire on the garage floor's hard surface. At least we knew that much.

Like a swat team, the two of us searched the car for the jack and spare tire to no avail. Finally, my husband discovered the jack. Located in a cleverly camouflaged compartment behind the second row seat, it consisted of four skinny pipes that looked like Tinker Bell's wand had been in a fight and lost.

My husband and I looked at each other in dismay. How the heck did this contraption fit together and where in the world did it jack up the car?

It was time to pull out the owner's manual.

Oh the shame of it, the shame! What dignified, self-respecting person ever reads the owner's manual? And while I am at it, whatever happened to the good old days when a jack was a jack?

In our defense, we are not tire-changing neophytes. We changed our first tire together as dating teenagers on another deserted Wisconsin road in the middle of a forest with only the starlight to guide us. We found the escapade hilarious; my parents understandably did not.

In addition, I am a veteran witness to tire-changing, having grown up in the 1950s when my family of seven experienced a tire blowout on virtually every annual summer vacation to the Northwoods and back that I can remember.

Sooner or later on our 450-mile odyssey, the familiar thumpity-thump-thump would resound through the open windows of our packed-to-the-brim station wagon with a canoe on top. With a few swears under his breath, my father would deftly pull the car to the side of an empty country road where a cluster of cows served as our only company.

But we didn't panic. We had this tire-changing nailed, so to speak. Our biggest challenge was to untie the canoe from the top of the car and unload all the luggage and vacation paraphernalia from the back end of the station wagon in order to retrieve the jack and spare.

Back then, even kids knew the spare tire's location; all jacks basically looked the same and always fit next to the wheel well; and no one needed an owner's manual to assemble them, nor was there one even if you'd wanted it.

With a few good cranks of the jack, that car rose up faster than a phoenix out of the ashes. A couple good twists of the wrench and the bolts came flying off. On went the spare, back went the bolts, back went the belongings and the canoe, and we were back on the road in a matter of hours. Child's play.

Unfortunately, the old adage "Don't fix what ain't broken" got overlooked in the computer-age tire tune-up department.

And so I have to admit, we opened the owner's manual to the index and looked up "jack," page 342. In a flat and halting voice that sounded like Frankenstein's, I slowly read the instructions out loud to my husband.

"Assemble the jack and jacking tools as shown. Connect jack handle driver (A) to two extensions (B), then to the lug wrench (C)."

Now, ours is not a fancy car. It is a basic American-made model, a medium-sized SUV, but I'll be danged if we couldn't identify the axle where we were instructed to fit the jack because there was so much metal hanging beneath the carriage of the car.

Before long, we two grandparents, college educated with master's degrees, were slithering under the car on the sandy garage floor like a couple of snakes.

"I think I've found it!" I shouted. "Look at this picture on page 344. It matches!"

We were so happy, you'd think we'd won the lottery.

Luckily, in our search beneath the car, we also discovered the spare tire. What genius decided to hide it down there is beyond me because our next quandary was how to disengage it. Back to the owner's manual, page 340.

"The spare tire is stowed under the rear of the vehicle by means of a cable winch mechanism. To remove or stow the spare, use the jack handle to rotate the 'spare tire drive' nut. The nut is located under a plastic cover at the center-rear of the cargo floor area, just inside the lift gate opening."

There you have it. Easy as pie.

As a bonus, there were enough CAUTION! warnings surrounding every direction that I felt I was entering Bill O'Reilly's No Spin Zone.

Somehow we figured it out, and slowly, slowly the spare tire floated down beneath the car like a spaceship twirling in an outer galaxy. Our sense of being in the twilight zone was complete.

Eventually, we accomplished our task. The manual's parting note was to stow the tire "beauty" side up. This must have been an inside joke, because, believe me, if there was a beauty side to that tire, I failed to recognize it.

Gratefully, we were soon back on the road to town where the nice tire man informed us that our flat tire was ruined. When he replaced the spare a few days later, I watched in wonder as he whipped that tire off and put on the new one in a matter of minutes.

Of course, he was using a power jack that could have shot our two-ton car to the moon. I've put one on my Christmas list.

Yet, like all good nightmares, mine was not over. Recently, I bought a car seat for my two infant granddaughters. After a few mind-boggling attempts to connect it properly, I was beginning to think tire changing looked easy.

As frustrated as a two-year-old and in fear of going ballistic, I once again succumbed to the instruction manual. Imagine my horror when I read:

"Check vehicle owner's manual for the vehicle top tether anchor locations. They may be identified using one of the anchor's symbols (Fig. b or Fig. c)."

Pass the Tylenol.

Downward Dogs

Lithe and limber we are not.

What we are is middle-aged. Our backs ache, our knees are sore, our energy wanes. We no longer spring out of our cars or up from chairs. We are stiff.

Our answer to a simple "Hi, how are you?" turns into a dissertation that makes the listener think we are earning a PhD in aches and pains. We are starting to whine.

This is not a good thing.

And so, in an effort to stave off this aging process, we flock to the gym, the pool, our bikes, and other such options in a desperate attempt to stay young, healthy, and strong. In the process, a myriad of Baby Boomers are discovering and espousing the benefits of yoga.

I decided to check it out.

Although my best friend from seventh grade has been practicing yoga for over thirty years, I have never given it much thought. Perhaps I now know why she is such a constantly calm and positive person who is still lithe and limber. I should have paid more attention.

In my belated quest for such attributes, I raced out and purchased a yoga book and headed off to class. I was in for a surprise. Having come from the Jane Fonda generation that needed to bounce and "feel the burn, baby!" I soon realized that yoga is an entirely different experience.

At this age, I am foremost and exceedingly grateful that the workout attire has changed. Back in my wild jump-up-and-down aerobic days, we women typically wore the de rigueur fashion of the era: form-fitting leotards and tights that disclosed to the world all of the features that we were desperately trying to hide.

Thankfully, today's yoga attire is looser and longer—mostly stretchy pants and simple T-shirts. Best of all, those heavy, tight aerobic shoes are history. Bare feet are the norm. Already my toes are happy.

For a person who hates exercise machines, I was thrilled with the prospect of using only a simple mat for equipment. Also, yoga does not involve the hard pumping music of yore, but rather mild and mellow instrumental tunes playing softly in the background and calling for relaxation.

After all, who wants to work up a sweat? Not me, I can assure you. Yet, soon I was twisting where I'd never twisted before.

One of the first aspects of practicing yoga is learning how to breathe. Since I'd been doing it for well over half a century, I thought I had breathing down. The correct way during yoga, however, is deep inhales and exhales through the nose and coordinated with each new stretch and movement. Instead of soothing my nervous system, however, breathing out or in at the right time was a struggle that just about made me hyperventilate.

I reminded myself to calm down. After all, this is yoga. It's been around for thousands of years, and its popularity is only growing. Clearly this is no passing fad like my Jane Fonda aerobics tapes. From *Om Yoga: A Guide to Daily Practice* by Cyndi Lee, I have learned that yoga "invites us to harmonize our body, breath, and mind as a way to experience wakefulness and compassion in our daily lives." Sounds better than a treadmill any day.

Lee goes on to say that "the path of hatha yoga involves physical exercises that enhance our cardiovascular system, strengthen our muscles, improve our digestive activity, and cleanse our entire body.... It also includes breathing exercises that soothe our nervous system and meditation that develops mental clarity." What's not to like?

My next challenge, however, was keeping up with the series of poses and their descriptive names. Warrior, cat, corpse, and cobra sound downright scary, and if I hear the command for downward dog one more time, I might start barking.

Full moon, five star, and child's pose are more to my liking. One of the best things I have discovered about yoga is that it's not about big muscles or perfect figures. As the instructor explained, it's more about centering yourself in the moment and letting go of competition, not only with others but also with yourself.

Ignoring that wisdom on my first day of class, I couldn't help but sneak an upside-down look through the triangle of my legs to see who else was in the class. I was amazed at the variety. There were men and women of all shapes, sizes, and ages. The woman directly in front of me was white haired and older than me, but definitely stronger and more limber.

I was impressed. I was also surprised to discover it's a much tougher workout than I thought. Perhaps that is why I like the corpse pose the best. Coming at the end of the session, it lives up to its name by simply requiring us to lie flat on the floor as if we are dead while the instructor encourages us to let go of the angst and anxieties of the day, freeing our minds for peace and harmony.

And the finest part is that at the end of the class, everyone rolls up smiling, visibly refreshed and renewed. Our muscles are stretched, our backs are more limber, and our spirits are calm. In my mind, it's a much better workout than jumping up and down or using a machine. My only worry is that the corpse pose, music, and soothing words are so relaxing that I will be tempted to fall asleep.

If that's the case, wake me only if I snore.

Cross-Country Skiing

I love the idea of it. Swishing through the still, snowy woods. Gliding past frosted trees on a pair of cross-country skis like a skater in sync with "The Blue Danube" waltz.

But that is not my reality. At least, not yet.

As a novice in the sport of cross-country skiing, I wobble down each small slope and shuffle awkwardly back up like a marionette controlled by jerking strings. I huff and I puff and I fall down, usually in an embarrassing position.

"Honey, this is not the time or place," my husband jokes from the top of a hill.

"Cut the wise cracks," I laugh with gasping breath. "Just get back here and help me up. I'm stuck."

So much for effortlessly gliding through the woods. This is hard work.

It's twenty-five degrees, and I'm starting to sweat. I never sweat.

We are new to this sport, and, at well past middle age, perhaps we are a little late to start. My husband's athletic agility, it must be said, gives him a distinctive edge. He circles endlessly up and back on the trail, checking patiently on my progress while I lumber along.

In fact, one woman skier at the trailhead sees him approach and apologizes for staring, saying she mistook him for her friend.

"He must not be a very good skier then," my husband says, referring humbly to his own efforts.

"Actually, he is quite a strong skier," she replies, swooshing past me down the hill that I am chugging up.

Beaming, my husband recounts this conversation for me as I stagger to the top. I'd pelt his smug smile with a snowball if only I had any strength left.

But hey, the latest scientific research verifies that healthy hearts make healthy brains, so I'm ready to give it a shot. Who says middle-agers can't strut their stuff? Not that there's a lot of stuff to strut, but we're working on it.

First of all, we got the skis. The result of a year-end sale, don't you know. Snazzy red. I feel like Dorothy in the Wizard of Oz Woods.

Next, after noticing that we looked like a pair of lumberjacks off to chop down some trees, we bought new outfits. Away with the jeans, flannel shirts, and vests, and on with loose Lycra in slimming black.

Gosh, we're looking good. Now, if I could only ski.

At least when we greet our fellow skiers, we will look the part. Thankfully, they are mostly a friendly group, these Nordic skaters, and not prone to snubbing beginners. Because I am often catching my breath after an arduous penguin-waddle to the top of a hill (where my husband stands awaiting me), we look like official trail greeters.

"Good morning!" I pant to our fellow skiers as they sweep serenely by.

"Beautiful day!" they shout back, easily swooping over hill and dale like colorful birds on a joyride through the forest.

We watch them disappear, their sleek muscles propelling them up and over the next rise. Dutifully, we take note of their strides, the swing of their arms, their pull and their push, hoping to learn by imitation.

They come in all shapes and ages: little girls with bright smiles moving like giddy fairies, gray-haired elders gliding with grace, and powerful young men and women at the peak of their form. At this time of year, it is obvious that some of the skiers sharing the trail with us are training for the American Birkebeiner. Skiers from all over the world come to the Hayward/Cable area in Wisconsin to test their stamina in this grueling fifty-one-kilometer cross-country race each February. They face forest trails studded with slippery downhill slopes and punishing uphill climbs that require control, speed, and endurance. And with any luck, there's a lot of good snow.

These competitors (of all ages) are a marvel of form and fitness, skiing with an ease and finesse that belie the exertion that will be required of them on race day. Lumbering along at my snail's pace, I can hardly fathom it.

Despite the rigors of the sport, many on the trail take time to greet each other, and their cheerful salutations ring through the woods like the echoes of a happy song.

Then there is silence. And that is the part I like best.

Weary muscles give me a chance to stop, look, and listen. Deer hooves dot the trail as if they too have enjoyed its early morning grooming; a bird's nest capped with a snowy hat perches on a tree branch, waiting for spring's thaw; woodland creatures poke their heads out of cozy homes in forest roots; a crow caws; and snowflakes fall all about me like angel dust.

Peace prospers.

But as Robert Frost so eloquently stated,

The woods are lovely, dark, and deep,
But I have promises to keep,
And miles to go before I sleep,
And miles to go before I sleep.

He wasn't kidding. It will be nightfall if I keep on at this pace. (In fact, some of these trails are lit at dusk, offering an intriguing invitation on a starry night.)

I push on, however, knowing the rewards of a warm fire, a good book, and yes, perhaps some "energy-renewing" chocolate await me.

Despite the achy muscles and my slow-as-a-porcupine style, I'm possessed to hit the trails again. For each outing brings a little more distance, a smoother glide, and fewer falls.

Who knows? Perhaps with a few lessons, I too might be swooshing through the forest like an owl on a moonlit night. I love the idea of it. And like any good dream, that's enough to make me want to try again.

Bum Knee

It's a bummer having a bum knee. I don't like it one bit. For some foolish reason, I thought I could glide down frosty cross-country ski trails and prance across their icy parking lots with the ease of a gazelle.

I forgot how old I was.

But I was quickly reminded of that fact after two hard falls on the ski trails and a third fall on the parking lot of the Happy Hooker Bait and Tackle Shop. It didn't help matters that all three falls occurred on the same day.

I had gone to the Happy Hooker (a Northwoods convenience store) to get a sweatshirt and hat bearing the store's moniker as a gag gift for my husband's sixtieth birthday.

I was so pleased with myself for purchasing this silly surprise that I all but skipped across the ice to my car. Bad mistake.

As the good book of Proverbs says, "Pride goeth before a fall," and down I went, right on my knee. I think that's the fall that did it. But amazingly, I didn't seem to be any worse for the wear.

It wasn't until about a month later when I returned to that snowy Northwoods area that I tempted fate again. (I should have headed south like everyone else.)

As if someone had pushed the replay button, I slipped while cross-country skiing and again on our icy driveway. Although I

was successful in not falling, my efforts to remain upright were
the straws that broke the camel's back. Or in this case, knee.

Standing in our driveway after my last slip, I suddenly found
I couldn't walk. Worse than the excruciating pain was the realization that my leg wouldn't do what it had always done. I
was stunned.

Attempting to overcome the pain and panic, I focused on the
sky. Standing on one leg, I looked up at the pearly clouds zipping
across a brilliant blue backdrop. The tips of tall emerald pines
swayed in the breeze. In that moment, I was profoundly reminded
of the fragility of all aspects of life, including the marvelous gift
of walking.

Eventually calmed by the sky's beauty, I somehow managed
to hop across our slippery, snowy driveway on one foot and drag
myself up the stairs.

To make a long story short, a visit to the emergency room
determined that I had a severe knee sprain. I left with instructions
to ice my knee, stay off it, take pain meds, and visit an orthopedic
doctor when I returned home.

And so here I sit several months later awaiting scheduled
knee surgery.

Gratefully, I have rarely been ill in my life, but I have been
the caregiver in numerous situations for loved ones, so this is a
complete role reversal for me. I am learning many things.

I am not used to asking for help or being waited on, and I'm
finding there is something quite humbling in having to do so. I
feel guilty not being able to do things for myself and having to de-
pend on others (though my husband says I'm getting quite good
at pointing my cane at him with directions). *Please* has become
the operative word.

It is also hard to be patient. Walking has always been my

favorite exercise. Especially now that it is spring, with the yellow forsythia in bloom, birdsong in the air, and buds bursting forth on bushes and trees like tiny butterflies with peridot wings on a branch, it is exasperating being unable to charge out into the sunshine for a brisk walk. Take away my other favorite activities, biking and dancing, and you have one frustrated gal.

Yet, I am also learning there is a peacefulness to being still. Unable to drive, I can't attend committee meetings, go to the grocery store, run errands, or attend to other family responsibilities. The rhythm of the day has shifted to a slower pace.

Propping my leg up outside so I could breathe some fresh air, I have witnessed the awakening of spring that I otherwise would have missed: the croaking call of a sandhill crane soaring high overhead, the dizzying dance of honey bees hovering over a patch of blue scilla, the sound of peeper frogs peeping, the flash of red from a scarlet tanager on his way north, and two newly hatched iridescent green-and-gold dragonflies chasing each other in a zigzagging flight.

Being stuck in a chair, I initially thought I'd go crazy needing this or that, but I soon discovered there's really very little I need. I have clothes in the closet, food in the cupboard, plenty of books and projects to keep me content, and the gift of time to reflect on simple everyday joys.

I am also learning to respect more acutely the courage and perseverance of those with mobility disabilities due to illness, accidents, old age, or the ravages of war. Their resilience and fortitude serve as everyday heroic reminders for us all.

But most of all, I am learning to appreciate small acts of kindness from family and friends. A phone call, a card, a ride to lunch, a visit with flowers—these things not only lift my spirits but allow me to experience the simple goodness of human nature.

Mother Theresa was right when she encouraged others to perform small acts with great love. As the recipient of these heartfelt gifts, I know what a difference they make.

Luckily, my knee injury is not too serious and, after surgery, I hope to regain my strong gait. When I do, I'll look forward to passing on those small acts of kindness to others.

And I'll do so, one very grateful step at a time.

Grateful Hearts

Put your hand in mine and let us help one another to see things better.

—CLAUDE MONET

Christmas Rose

"He's drunk," my brother whispered as we watched my father stagger up the snowy path to our back door. We peeked through the window as he fumbled with the few small packages in his hands while trying to find the doorknob. With a push the door flew open and he lurched in, bringing the snow and wind of the Christmas Eve night with him.

"Merry Christmas, Daddy!" shouted the five of us children in cheerful chorus.

He looked up with somewhat startled eyes that struggled to focus on each of us.

"Bah, humbug," he replied, part in jest, part in truth.

We all laughed nervously.

We didn't need this moment to know it wasn't going to be a good Christmas. That was already obvious. With my father out of work and five kids to feed and clothe, there were no presents under the tree, and we'd already checked the usual hiding places.

Christmas Eve looked bleak. But it hadn't always been that way.

We'd had plenty of Christmases with presents flowing out from under the tree and brimming around the hearth. There were Lionel trains for my two brothers and beautiful Marshall Field's dolls for us three girls. Once there was a toboggan and another year a canoe. Who would have guessed that bountiful Christmases would not have continued?

Certainly not my father. He had been raised to believe his father's company would one day be his. But a string of circumstances that included his father's untimely death and his own absenteeism while serving overseas in World War II resulted in a change in controlling powers. As is often the case with children of family-owned businesses and outside partners, there was conflict.

Unfortunately, at age forty-five with five kids and a mortgage, my father found out the hard way that the controlling powers no longer wanted him around. They fired him. And it came as quite a blow, as the son of the original owner. It would take seven years of financial reversal, a series of short-lived jobs, and the onslaught of alcoholism before he finally made it back on his feet.

But on this Christmas Eve, we children understood none of this. We only knew we wanted presents and a sober father, and neither seemed in sight.

Nevertheless, my mother carried on with her usual optimistic fortitude. She salt-and-peppered a roast and stuck it in the oven, rolled out the dough for her homemade rolls, and filled the Santa punch bowl with eggnog dashed with nutmeg. At least we knew that our stockings hung by the small, flickering fire would be filled by morning with oranges and hard candy.

And so we settled in for a night of nothing. Each of us retreated to a quiet corner of the house, nursing our dashed hopes for the presents we had longed for and worrying about what we would tell our friends when they asked what we got for Christmas.

A short while later, my father called us from our personal reveries back to the living room.

"Nancy, Marnie, David, Tommy, and Mary, please come here," he said quietly.

As we filed in, we saw on the dining room table a single, small present waiting for each of us.

My father handed them to us one by one, and we eagerly opened our gifts. I believe my brothers received silver pocket watches that had been our grandfather's, but I'm not sure because, as a self-absorbed teenager, I was focused only on what my one present could be.

Slowly, I opened the clumsily wrapped box. Framed against soft cotton lay a pin of two carved ivory roses on a golden stem. My sisters and mother had varying versions: one pin with three roses, one rose necklace, and one huge single rose, which we think was meant for my mother but, due to my father's drunkenness, was given to my little sister by mistake.

"Merry Christmas," my father said simply.

When I looked up, I could see the failure in his sad, green eyes.

"I wish it could be more," he added. "But that's all I can do."

We thanked him with hugs and kisses. Although my pin wasn't what a selfish teenage girl coveted, I could sense my father's genuine sorrow.

For what could be worse than coming home nearly empty-handed on Christmas Eve to a wife and five expectant children? Surely, his misery was great, enough so that a stop at the local tavern provided the numbness he needed to face us.

Reflecting back on that Christmas Eve so long ago, I find that my experience as a parent has altered my perspective. Through the prism of time, I look up once again into my father's gentle eyes and see something else besides the sadness. It is his hope for forgiveness.

In these simple gifts of white roses, a flower he always loved, he longed for us to see beyond his failure, his alcoholism, his despair. Somewhere behind all the frustrated ugliness was a father full of kindness, humor, patience, and, yes, wisdom. If only we all could believe it, perhaps he could, too.

Despite our various ages at the time, between six and sixteen, I think all five of us children sensed and felt this. It is not a Christmas Eve held in darkness, but rather one of enlightening love.

And so I wear my Christmas rose pin not only on that eve of starlit expectation, but throughout the year as a symbol of the strength and courage it takes to overcome personal struggles. It reminds me to seek the hope, find the goodness, and look beyond the despair of those who are troubled.

It was my father's most precious gift to me.

Giving Thanks

It all starts with the cranberry sauce.

Bubbling and popping on the stove, the round berries shoot tiny splatters of ruby fireworks, announcing with their sweet scent that it's Thanksgiving Eve. They are the kickoff to Turkey Day, igniting an excitement for the fine food, family, and fellowship that are to follow.

The cranberry sauce tradition began with my father, who used to stand in the kitchen with a pack of Lucky Strikes on the counter and a cigarette in hand, stirring his cranberry concoction into the late hours of the night. We five children drifted off to sleep with its bittersweet fragrance filling the air, accompanied by the clanking sound of dishes being washed, and awoke to the smoky smell of turkey in the oven.

The role of the cranberry chef landed in my lap twenty-four years ago on a snowy Christmas Eve as I cooled a sick baby with a 104-degree temperature in a tepid bath and shouted downstairs to my sister-in-law to start mashing the potatoes.

Later, as I waited for the doctor to call back, I stirred the gravy with one arm and rocked my fretful son with the other. Suddenly, I announced that I wasn't hosting Christmas anymore. I said I'd take Thanksgiving, which seemed less stressful than trying to cook, wrap presents, and prepare for Santa's arrival with excited (or sick) little ones waiting in the wings.

My angelic sister-in-law rose to the occasion and magnani-
mously offered to take over the hosting duties for Christmas. And
so, twenty-four years later, I have a fine collection of pilgrims,
turkeys, and corn decorations, and she has a myriad of pine-
patterned plates and Santa Clauses. We are set for life.

Over the years our family has developed a host of Thanksgiving traditions that would be harder to change than the position
of the North Star.

My brother always brings his original recipe for stuffed mush-
rooms, our mother's famous appetizer loaf that we call Cheese
Whiz, and our grandmother's 1920s recipe for creamed onions.
My brother-in-law arrives carrying homemade pecan, pumpkin,
and cherry pies with fluted crusts still warm from the oven. An adopted "uncle" bustles in with his signature sweet potatoes swimming in an ocean of brown sugar and butter. These men can cook.

Each year, I serve the pièce de résistance: my mother's overnight yeast-rising dinner rolls. With all the time, energy, and flying
flour involved, they are an act of love. Throw in the stuffed turkey,
mashed potatoes, gravy, and a vegetable (for appearances), and
we are as content as a family of partridges in a pear tree.

Our Thanksgiving feast begins as we join hands in prayer
around the table and say in turn what we are especially grateful for this year. Sometimes the blessings are simple, as when
my then ten-year-old son gave sincere thanks for pumpkin pie.
Sometimes they are emotional thanks for good health or the joy
of having a new bride at our table. Always they are poignant and
from the heart.

After dinner and dishes, my husband starts playing Christmas
carols on the piano, which is our cue to gather in the living room,
grab a song sheet, and kick off the season with carols.

Our show-stopping favorite is "The Twelve Days of Christmas," where we all vie to sing one of the days as a solo (or duet,
depending on voice confidence). For years, my brother-in-law

laid claim to the fifth day of Christmas and the five golden rings, which he dished up in a variety of melodious interpretations on each round, sending us into peals of laughter and applause. Lately, however, he has bowed out of this role and younger voices are testing it out.

Our Thanksgiving Day activities are so traditional they run like a script.

"It's always the same," one of my three sons laughingly said last year. "Nothing ever changes."

"Oh, but it will," I answered with a smile. "And then one day you'll say 'Remember when...'"

For our sons are starting to marry and other families and places will beckon. Old traditions will fade away, some may stay, and new ones will surely be added. It is all good.

Twenty-nine years ago, my father was battling acute leukemia. In anticipation of another round of chemotherapy treatments in a Chicago hospital, he prepared his cranberry sauce a week ahead of time, simmering it on the stove until it was just the right thickness and then freezing it with the hope that he would join us for the festivities.

When Thanksgiving Day arrived with its sunny promise of bringing everyone together, my father decided his treatment wasn't progressing quickly enough for his "escape" from the hospital. So, unbeknownst to his nurses, he took matters into his own hands and sped things up by making the chemo drip faster. Back home, we gladly held off on our feast, hour by hour, as we eagerly waited for news of his release.

It wasn't until the golden-red glow of a prairie sunset filled the little living room of our first home that he and my mother, who had driven the hour into Chicago and the hour back to pick him up, finally arrived. Pale and weak, he walked through our front door with the biggest grin on his face and the cranberry sauce in hand. No gift could have been finer.

Gathering around the table in the soft glow of candlelight, we held hands as I read an ancient Native American prayer that ends with these lines:

All is more beautiful,
All is more beautiful,
And life is thankfulness.
These guests of mine
Make my house grand.

We all sensed that it would be my father's last Thanksgiving, and it was. In that moment of tender grace, there seemed no better prayer.

~

My Father's Thanksgiving Eve Cranberry Sauce

5 cups fresh cranberries
1 cup sugar
1 cup water

Mix all ingredients together in a saucepan and bring to a slow boil over low heat. Continue to simmer for one and a half or two hours, stirring occasionally as needed until sauce has thickened to desired consistency. Sprinkle with a dash of cinnamon or nutmeg. Savor the scents. Cool and place in refrigerator overnight. Serve with turkey and all the trimmings the next day. Enjoy!

Swinging along the Open Road

I'm the driver. My eighty-year-old mother sits in the passenger seat of her aging compact car. The trunk is crammed, and the back seat is piled high with assorted bags, boxes, and luggage for an extended summer stay in Wisconsin's Northwoods.

This is the first time in the sixty-two years that my mother has been going up to our family's 1929 log cabin that she has asked for assistance with the 450-mile drive from Illinois. She has already driven the equivalent distance from Ohio by herself to get to this point.

"It's the beginning of a new era," she says as we pull out of my driveway into the early morning sunlight.

She should know. She has lived through a lot of eras in the years she has spent on our cabin's lovely wooded hilltop.

There was the courting era with my father, when his family asked my mother and her parents and sister to spend a month with them on the lake in the summer of 1938. There was their era as newlyweds, when my father and mother drove up with another couple in the fall of 1946 after my father's return from World War II, seeking the beauty and peacefulness of the forest.

There was the era of the children, all five of us growing up in raucous splendor on the water's edge. This was followed by the era of grown children and learning to live alone as a widow. Finally, the era of laughing, romping grandchildren arrived. Now they too are grown, and that era has come to an end as well.

As we begin our day's journey, my mother turns to me with her ever-optimistic approach to change and says, "The one thing about a long car ride is it gives you a chance for a good visit."

And so that is exactly what we do. Over the course of our eight-hour drive, we discuss family, friends, health, and the lake adventures we'll share upon arrival.

Of course, there was no time for a good visit when my mother drove the five of us kids Up North. Because my father often had to work, she was the sole driver. Packed in a 1959 station wagon with a canoe strapped on top and the back end piled to the roof with luggage, we rode three to the second seat, three to the front. Hot wind blew through the rolled-down windows and across our sweaty faces.

We made frequent roadside stops, either to use the old enamel car potty or to accommodate a carsick sibling who had to up-chuck. When it was time to stop for gas, it took ten minutes for us to find and unscramble the shoes and socks we had kicked off. We were always hungry, so our mother appeased us with green grapes and chunks of cheddar cheese. And, of course, with five kids on such a long car ride, we fought.

"Stop leaning on me!"

"You smell!"

"Who stole my gum?"

A whiff of Juicy Fruit breath would soon divulge the culprit.

To combat these periods of crabbiness, my mother demanded we sing. It is not easy to get five feisty kids to burst into song, and yet she insisted.

So, sing we did. Old hymns, scout songs, campfire favorites, whatever each of us knew. "Swinging along the Open Road" was a scout song I loved and one that we sang often. When we de-scended into the epic hilarity of "Ninety-Nine Bottles of Beer on the Wall" or "Found a Peanut, Found a Peanut . . . ," my mother commanded a halt and moved us on to the license plate game.

Inevitably on our Northwoods journey, car trouble struck. Sooner or later the engine overheated or the sudden rumble of a wobbly wheel signaled a flat tire. Once again, we would pull over into the waving wildflowers of the roadside.

In order for the engine to be examined or the spare tire to be retrieved, the canoe had to be taken off the top of the car and the entire luggage unpacked from the backseat. This took quite a while as my father always tied masterful, complicated scout knots to keep the canoe from sliding off, and somehow the five of us kids always managed to stuff enough junk into the back end that the roadside eventually looked like a spontaneous garage sale.

Help came in a variety of forms. Sometimes a farmer in the fields ambled over and helped change a tire. Occasionally, patrons of a quirky, nearby Northwoods bar took a look under the hood as we waited inside the tavern, intrigued by the mingled scents of smoke and beer. Once, a dear friend drove one hundred miles round trip in the middle of the night to fetch us.

A few times, the trouble was severe enough that we had to spend the night in the nearest lodging. This usually turned out to be a rundown motel where the bathroom was down the hall and the bedbugs were holding a convention.

Yet my tireless mother remained undaunted throughout this odyssey. When we finally arrived at the cabin, it was often past midnight. She still had the job of unpacking and making beds. Although we older kids could help, the overall responsibility was hers. Some would never have attempted this road trip alone, yet she seemed to thrive on the adventure of it all.

And so, on this sunny summer morning, another era begins. We are reversing roles. My mother and I assume our new roles without complaint. I am the official "cab driver," happy to have the opportunity to provide a lift. She is the passenger, a little more tired, a little less steady on her feet, accepting the ride with grace. She looks on the bright side. It is a new adventure.

As she predicted, we do have a good visit. We eat green grapes and cheddar cheese. We do not have car trouble. We sing.

Dancing with Vera

The woods and water beckon. Even though the two ladies are in their late eighties, summer in Wisconsin's Northwoods calls to them like the Siren songs of ancient mythology. The urge to go is strong. And so we do.

I am their chauffeur.

One of them is my mother, Woody, who has traveled to this same northern lake for over sixty-eight years. The other is her dear friend, Vera, who has made the identical journey for fifty-eight years. Rarely has either missed a summer.

The two women met as newly married brides in the early days of World War II and have been friends ever since—their lives intertwined by business, church, children, and, of course, the lake.

Now both are widowed and, due to various physical ailments, including failing eyesight, they are no longer able to make the nearly 450-mile trip alone. When I made a spontaneous offer to be the designated driver, as I'd been for my mother several summers earlier, they gratefully accepted.

We're taking off on an early midsummer morning in the midst of a downpour. As I load the car with my mother's walker, thunder and lightning boom and flash around us.

"It only adds to our adventure!" says Vera, who still plays golf and frequently whistles a merry tune.

My ladies are happy, happy. They chatter the entire eight hours that it takes to get us Up North. There is much reminiscing, especially since both families now have fifth generations coming up to the lake this summer.

They remember when the cabins were lit only by kerosene lamps; the wooden fishing boats ran on three-and-a-half horsepower motors; the drive took two days on gravel roads; and skunks, porcupines, and bears were common sightings.

But mostly they remember the traditions, funny moments, and special times shared with many friends and family members over six decades on the lake.

"Do you want to stay on the interstate or take the old way?" I ask.

"Oh, the old way!" exclaims Vera. "It's much more woodsy and beautiful."

I turn off the interstate onto a two-lane highway that weaves through familiar rural towns, fields studded with rolls of harvested golden wheat, faded red barns, and cheery gardens. Woody and Vera gaze out the window, savoring every mile as the trees multiply to become forests and flashes of bright blue lakes sparkle in welcome.

As we near my family's log cabin in the woods, an almost palpable sense of anticipation fills the car. The winding curves of the road and the leafy green tunnels of the arching trees begin to take on a heartwarming familiarity. Even though my mother's eyesight is greatly diminished, she recognizes that we are almost there.

"Isn't this exciting, Vera?" she asks.

"I'm just taking in all the old sights," Vera replies with a sigh.

Finally, we're there. Woody and Vera are giddy as we open the door to each little room of the cabin and finally enter the cherished porch overlooking the lake. And then the fun begins.

There is no sitting around in rocking chairs for these ladies. Word soon spreads around the lake that returning royalty has arrived, and they're off, a pair of social butterflies with me along for the ride.

If you have never ridden to a Friday night fish fry with five octogenarians in a 1987 Oldsmobile station wagon, you've missed a joyride that could rival any teenagers'. The laughter and chatter never stop. And that's just the start. No effort is too great. Woody and Vera snatch up every opportunity afforded them.

They make it down the many steps to the dock, attend the little white church in the vale, picnic on the patio, organize an afternoon bridge game, and dine on scrumptious grilled salmon at a dear friend's cabin, all in one day. Lake friends come calling on a continuous basis. We throw our own cocktail party for nineteen friends, and when a guest plays ragtime on our old upright piano, Vera grabs my hand for a spontaneous dance, such is her happiness.

On our last night, a friend generously takes the ladies out on her pontoon boat so they can see the lake once more. It is especially hard for my mother to get into the boat, but she finally makes it.

Coasting on the blue water in the shimmering sunlight of late afternoon, they take in all their beloved sights: the eagles' nest boasting two big eaglets, the loons bobbing, and the familiar islands that dot the water like emerald ships at sail.

As the warm wind blows across our bow, Vera and Woody grow quiet, their serene faces taking in all the surrounding beauty. Are they wondering if they'll ever pass this way again? Are memories of cherished friends and family, many of them now gone, washing over them like so many waves upon the shore?

All I know is that they have never dwelled on what might have been. Despite great heartbreak and sorrow in their lives and current physical struggles, they continue to savor each moment and to seek joy and optimism in every day that God gives them.

Some might say I was foolhardy to undertake such a trip, but as their chauffeur, I believe I soaked up some wisdom. As my ladies would attest, it's always about the journey. And my dance with Vera was worth every mile.

You've Got Mail

There are too many of them. Too many to sort. Too many to read. Too many to save.

And yet, they are a lifetime of letters. A cache of history spanning several generations that have been stashed in our family home for years, tucked into closets, corners of the garage, and any nook and cranny that would hold them. Boxes and boxes of them, overflowing with love and tears and joy and the activities of the times.

One batch came with us when our family moved to a new home in 1954. Over the years, more were added and remained in the house when my brother bought it from our widowed mother after she retired to Ohio.

Now fifty-four years after we bought it, the house is leaving our family; my brother is selling it and moving away. It is time for the letters to move as well. But what to do with them? None of us realized how many had been saved. Out of sight, out of mind.

As my brother kept uncovering boxes and boxes of letters, the task of sorting through them became almost overwhelming. One look at the musty cardboard containers and dust-covered letters, and practical folks would have pitched them without a second thought.

But we have never been a practical clan. Our creative curiosity got the better of us, and we began to take a peek.

Amazingly, our random picks seemed uncannily appropriate, as though the letters were still speaking to us all these many years later.

As my mother and I sat at the kitchen table in the light of the early summer sun, we began to examine the contents of one of the boxes. The first letter I pulled out was written years ago by my mother's sister, and because my eighty-eight-year-old mother can no longer see well, I read it to her.

It was filled with good cheer and the happy chatter that my aunt, now deceased, so often included in letters over the decades to her sister living three states away.

"Oh, how I have been longing to hear from my sister," my mother said, "and here is a letter from her, like it was written yesterday."

That was only the beginning.

Here was a long letter from my grandfather to my father on his twenty-first birthday in 1936, officially welcoming him to manhood. In it he wished his son happiness in the years ahead, offered up wisdom for life, congratulated him on meeting some secret goal between the two of them, and sent him into the future with endless love and devotion.

No wonder my father kept it.

Here was a 1944 love letter from my mother to my father overseas during World War II, describing her day, making plans for the year ahead, and lovingly longing for his return.

Here were boxes of get-well letters from friends and family to my maternal grandmother in 1953, offering her courage and faith in her struggle with cancer, and a follow-up box of sympathy cards upon her death.

Soon the boxes of letters began to move into the next generation, giving insight into my siblings' and my growing-up years. Thankfully, my younger sister arrived on the scene to help out.

She found a hilarious letter I'd written from camp in 1960

when I was about ten years old. It recounts a fellow camper's insistence that she "saw a great big round light way up in the sky and it would light up everything and would stay there for about five seconds ... I didn't see it because I had a headache and didn't want to see it." Another camper told me she saw a "man in a white suit and hat look in my window ... but I know it isn't true."

Apparently, I liked reporting interesting events at an early age.

Another fun find was a letter from my paternal grandmother in 1958 describing our stay at our cabin in northern Wisconsin. She writes to my parents that I am good about swimming at the lake only when older adults are around. However, I have a problem remembering the time, even though I have pinned my wristwatch to my beach robe.

"So you had trouble being on time even back then," remarked my husband, a prompt creature if there ever was one, who has put up with my lack of punctuality for our entire marriage.

Other discoveries included small books of love poems from my sister's boyfriend over forty years ago; endless business transactions, old wills, legal letters, résumés, and banking papers that unraveled some family mysteries and created others; joyful letters from friends sending welcomes to the newest baby in the family; news from aunts, uncles, cousins, fathers, mothers, and grandparents graced with good wishes of the day; and a remarkable memoir from an unknown great-uncle describing his family farm at the turn of the century and their oxen, Buck and Board, plowing the prairie.

Even my mother, the main keeper of the letters, muttered an "Egad!" as yet another box was hauled to the table to sort through. The question, of course, is why in the world they were kept all these years.

My brother-in-law, a history professor, remarked that it almost seems disrespectful to the writers to throw them away. We all agreed. After all, someone was thinking of a loved one, took the time to gather pen and paper, sit down and write, find a stamp, and post these letters in the mail, often timed to the mailman's schedule.

Nowadays, of course, letter writing has all but disappeared in favor of email, text messaging, and cell phone calls. And although these are the communications of the times, something is definitely missing: a paper trail of lives lived.

Despite the dusty work and the emotional roller coaster that these letters sent us on, the ones we randomly selected to read spoke to each of us as though they were meant to be discovered.

In truth, beneath the many laughs and funny finds there was an undercurrent of sadness. Life, we know, does not always turn out as we had anticipated. So many of the good wishes for joy and success written so lovingly to the letters' recipients did not come true. Failures, illness, death, financial misfortune, lost love, personal struggles, and various disappointments often occurred instead.

Despite the setbacks, however, there are a myriad of blessings. The writers continually express joy in everyday simplicities, humor, an awareness and appreciation of the natural world, and, most importantly, faith in the future.

These letters offer testimonies to lives lived fully and with the best of efforts no matter the circumstances. The strong bonds of love connecting family and friends are the things that make a difference.

Perhaps the ultimate message of these heartfelt missives is to open our hearts with faith to the paths of light and love that lie ahead.

No matter what comes our way, joy awaits.

Heaven in a Wildflower

Out of the cold dirt they come. Beneath the brown leaves, next to the gray rocks, beside the sculpted tree trunks, their colorful faces lift toward the light. Brilliant blues, egg-yolk yellows, and pale pinks welcome the warmth of spring's sunshine. They are back, these woodland wildflowers, like God's confetti upon the earth. And we of little faith wondered if they'd ever return. Enduring the cold gray winter made us feel as if we were stuck in a perennial snowbank.

Yet beneath the frigid ground, these little wonders lay in wait. And now that they are here, I know exactly what I must do. I call my mother.

"The blue scilla are in bloom!" I announce.

"Oh, we don't want to miss them!" she says.

She has been waiting for this call. After all, she is the one who passed her love of wildflowers on to me. So together we check the weather, pick a day, and postpone all our seemingly important business in order to see the wildflowers. As my mother says, "It is our thing."

Even at age eighty-eight, my mother's memory is filled with wildflower outings, like a virtual album of pressed blossoms.

In the 1920s, when my mother was growing up in the rolling hills of Ohio, soft spring days meant family excursions into the wooded countryside in search of trailing arbutus, a rare and fragrant flower that creeps along the ground, making for a perfect picnic spot.

When she moved to Illinois as a young wife and mother, she discovered Morton Arboretum near the village of Lisle. Each spring she frequently packed my siblings and me, a buggy, and a picnic into the car for a leafy stroll around the arboretum's winding paths. In one of my favorite pictures, I'm a plump eight-month-old baby plopped in a patch of daffodils, studying their golden trumpets with wide-eyed wonder.

For a lover of wildflowers, May Day provided the perfect excuse for my mother to haul her five kids out to a country road at the crack of dawn. There, amid the dewy grass, we picked wildflowers for the baskets we'd made the night before. Back home, we stuffed them to overflowing with our flowers, popcorn, and gumdrops, dashed to neighbors' houses to hang them on doorknobs, rang the bell, and ran home. All before school started.

I can't say we were very alert for our schoolwork that day, but we knew our wildflowers.

Not surprisingly, when it came time for my first major science project, I knew exactly what I wanted to do. My mother drove me back to Morton Arboretum, this time as a fourteen-year-old, and I explored, identified, and photographed all the blooming wildflowers I could find. It was my first attempt at nature photography, a love I still pursue.

Wildflowers, however, bloom for only a short time and fade fast. So for my mother—who can still recite Wordsworth's "Daffodils," memorized over eight decades ago—it is time to seize the day.

Like the wildflowers themselves, my mother and I have come full circle. Our roles are reversed, and just as she pushed me in a buggy, I will push her in a wheelchair in order to accomplish our mission.

"We're off to see the blue scilla!" she happily announces to her friends as I wheel her out the door of her retirement home.

"The what?" they ask.

"The blue scilla are blooming all over Fabyan Forest Preserve," she explains. "They are just gorgeous!"

With a wave we roll on by, no time for chatter. Beauty beckons.

My sister and my mother discovered the blue scilla some years back just by chance. They had gone there to picnic and found the woods and hillsides covered in a carpet of tiny blue flowers, perfuming the air with a delicate scent.

On this fine spring day, I unload her wheelchair from the car and roll my mother along the bike path in search of a perfect picnic spot. Easily finding one, we sit and admire the gently flowing river, greet passing bikers and hand-holding lovers, share our picnic lunches, and listen as birds serenade us with their happy spring songs.

Then, we move on to seek the scilla. Although they are all around us as I wheel my mother along, I must point them out to her. Legally she is blind. And although she can see somewhat, much is dimmed and diminished.

"Here's a patch," I say.

"Where?" she asks.

"Right beside you," I answer.

"Oh, how lovely!" she says, looking hard.

As I push her along, I point out our beloved bright daffodils and the hints of a magnolia tree's first white blossoms.

"To think that so many don't know about this beauty!" my mother says.

Pausing to rest on a hill, we gaze at a sun-dappled ravine filled with endless scilla bobbing in the breeze like a sea of blue butterflies. In that moment, we know exactly what the poet William Blake meant when he described seeing "heaven in a wild flower."

"I just want to be able to remember this sight forever," my mother says.

And so do I.

The return of the wildflowers signals a sense of rebirth and renewal, hope for new beginnings, and faith in unimagined possibilities on the horizon. In all of life's circumstances, my mother has continually sought beauty and, in doing so, finds the bliss so aptly expressed in her beloved Wordsworth poem: "And then my heart with pleasure fills, / And dances with the daffodils."

If I can remember those gifts of optimism, then as in the hymn of old, perhaps my soul too can sing.

In Search of a Silver Lining

The day we all dreaded had arrived. But there was no way around it.

No one wants to put a loved one in a nursing home. And, more importantly, no family member wants to live in one, least of all my mother.

For a widow who still loved visiting and partying with her family and friends and thrived on activity, even in a physically frail state at age eighty-nine, a nursing home was the last place she would have chosen.

It all started with a small stroke, and while she was recovering from that, a fall resulting in a snapped ankle sealed the deal. A wheelchair had become her permanent new friend. Because her retirement home provided unassisted living, there was no other decision my four siblings and I could make. Two of them lived on opposite coasts and the other two lived several hours away, and so I was the one in charge.

It was not a leadership role I cherished.

Yet, time was of the essence, as the Medicare clock that designates how many days a patient can stay in rehab care was ticking away. Her days were numbered. And so were mine. I needed to find a suitable nursing home fast.

Because money was an issue, our choices were limited. I had not been in a nursing home for a long time, and to say I was shocked the moment I walked into one would be a gargantuan understatement.

The first and closest nursing home I checked out was crowded and noisy. Televisions blared. Wheelchair-bound patients sat in slumped repose scattered all over the premises. Therapy dogs roamed the hallways, which was rather unsettling for a first-time visitor. The scents of urine, dogs, medicines, and nursing home food wafted through the air. Although this care facility had a reputation for being competent, I couldn't get out of there fast enough. I knew my mother would recoil as much as I did.

The second one was no better and had an opening only in an Alzheimer's wing until a bed in an appropriate area opened up. This for a woman who could still recite Shakespeare from memory and play a competitive hand of bridge?

The third was similar to the other two. The fourth was a strong possibility, but alas, no room at the inn.

At my wit's end, I was sliding into panic mode. Fatigue and worry were my constant companions. Where could she go? Coming to my home even for a short time with hired help was next to impossible due to its stairs and lack of a first-floor shower. Would I have to start looking for a nursing home out of our area?

And then what?

How would I visit her on a timely basis and manage her health care? Would I be isolating her even more from friends and family? More importantly, would she feel as though I had abandoned her? Thrown away the key, so to speak? Out of sight, out of mind? Guilt shackled my soul.

And then, by the grace of God, I was alerted to an opening in a nursing home twenty miles away. It was a place where several of my friends' parents had stayed, which was reassuring. Even so, I drove through the early morning traffic with trepidation in my heart, wondering what I would find.

The first thing that greeted me when I walked in the door was an oasis of living plants and flowers surrounding a small pond filled with goldfish. A path for wheelchairs ran around and over it with places to pause or for a visitor to pull up a chair. When I spotted a live turtle resting on the pond's raised rocks, I knew I had found my mother a home.

The staff was welcoming and friendly, and the fact that it had one of our favorite trees, the pine, in its name was the icing on the cake. With my siblings' approval, I signed on the dotted line.

Yet, the worst was not over.

A nursing home, no matter how clean or neat, is still a nursing home. Elderly patients still slept slumped in their wheelchairs; TVs blared the latest soap operas in the commons area; intercom announcements calling for staff reverberated down the halls; and the occasional, sudden shouts from an incoherent resident unsettled all within earshot.

Even as a visitor, it was easy to get depressed, and I wasn't even the one who would be living there. My mother was. And it was time to tell her.

But how could I ever tell her that she needed to move out of her beloved retirement home where a cast of friends, fun activities, loving staff, and great food had been her daily experience for the past four and a half years? How could I tell a woman who was keenly social, mentally sharp, attractively dressed, beautifully coiffed, and who still loved her lipstick, that she would be living in a shared room with only a bed, dresser, and tiny closet to call her own?

How could I tell her that she would share this small space with a roommate who was one hundred years old and totally deaf? How could I tell her that meals were assigned seating with folks who could barely feed themselves?

But most of all, how could I tell her how sorry I was to have to do all this? How could I tell her it was breaking my heart?

And yet, I did.

When the time came, she just closed her eyes and nodded. She knew it was coming. I held her hand and we were both silent for a moment.

She didn't cry. She never cried. Instead, she looked up and bravely sought a silver lining. She recounted all the good times we had had together since she had moved near to me four and a half years ago, thanking me for all that I had done, not only in finding a nursing home but assisting with her care at her retirement home: doctor's appointments attended, social outings planned, errands run, clothes managed, groceries gathered. All these occasions, though not always easy, had created times for us to be together. And now, especially at this turning point, we were both grateful for them.

"Happiness was ours," she said. A gift of grace.

It was just what I needed to hear.

And so, to the nursing home she went. Courageous and optimistic.

Although the home turned out to be the perfect place for her, it was a difficult year and a half of slow decline. Hospital stays, dialysis, heart trouble, and near-blindness eventually took their toll. Even so, she remained cheerful and mentally alert to the end.

Despite my best intentions, however, I was not with her when she died.

My fortieth anniversary was approaching, and my sister came up to stay with our mother so that my husband and I could celebrate at our beloved cabin in the Northwoods where we had spent our honeymoon. Before I left, my mother and I hugged goodbye amid the bright flowers and greenery of the nursing home's outdoor garden. She was happy that I was heading Up North and sent me off with her blessing.

Even so, leaving her was not easy. I had a feeling I would not see her again as I climbed into my car with a heavy heart and waved a final goodbye. As I headed down the road, I looked back in my side-view mirror to see my mother and sister sitting peacefully together in the warm June sunshine.

It is a memory I will always cherish.

She died unexpectedly the day before my anniversary, alone in an ambulance on the way to the hospital. I drove the eight hours home as soon as I heard the news and spent my anniversary picking out her casket with my brother, sister, and husband.

And yet, looking back, I knew my mother was grateful for those final days of life, for that extra time together. And so were my siblings and I.

Despite the many challenges and difficulties, or maybe because of them, we continually sought that silver lining and found it. No matter how dim or dark the days, some sun always broke through in the strong rays of our love for each other. And because of that, even in a nursing home, "happiness was ours."

Looking for Rainbows

Only a few are left. They are all but gone. Dave, Lucile, Franklin, Vi, George, Tommy, June, Sten, Bob, Woody, and Dick, among others, no longer greet us with their friendly smiles and hugs.

Like loons leaving the lake at the end of summer for distant shores, a cherished generation is drifting away one by one. For those of us who had the good fortune of vacationing with these older friends year after year, it is a mournful, melancholy time when we hear yet another has passed on.

There are many reasons we loved this Depression era and wartime generation, not the least of which are their Northwoods memories of a time before Jet Skis, boat lifts, and megamotors hit the scene. After all, this generation knew the simple pleasures of rowing to the rhythmic squeak of the oarlock, the purr of the 3½-horsepower motor, the golden glow of kerosene lamps.

They are the ones who knew the old love songs, like "Good Night, Irene" and "Shine On, Harvest Moon," and sang them with gusto around an old lodge piano or on a moonlit dock.

They are the ones who could easily identify the constellations, thrilled at the howl of the wolves, picnicked on the islands in the rain, and partied at each other's cabins at the drop of a hat. And no matter how often they heard the loons' flight songs fill the heavens with their harmony, they are the ones who always looked up.

Best of all, they could share these stories with us. And so, as these dear old friends depart the lake and the woods forever, they leave behind a great void. For who will remember? Who will share these simple pleasures of the past? Or perhaps, more importantly, who will care?

As children vacationing at our Northwoods family log cabin in the 1950s and 1960s, we found our parents' generation to be a huge part of the charm of coming to the lake. They were adults that we looked up to and admired, older friends who were always happy to see us.

And even though they were as old as our parents, or older, we never thought of them that way. When we grew into young adults, it seemed as though the age differences simply melted away. We were their peers. We saw each other as members of the same group of friends—people we looked forward to seeing every summer despite the thirty-year age gaps.

In fact, the age diversity simply enhanced the lake experience for us all. Whether we ran into each other at a fish fry, partied at each other's cabins, canoed down a river together, or waved to one another from our docks and boats, these older friends added a comforting sense of familiarity to our summer vacations.

In knowing them, we too learned the old love songs, the splendor of a walk through a virgin forest, the joy of organizing an island picnic, the simple pleasures of rowing. They were the ones we turned to with questions about the history of the area's wildlife, the people, the lakes, the forests. Not only did they have the answers, but with each retelling, they added a little personal history of their own.

Like the sparkling glacial boulder on the road near the cabin that greeted us each summer, this generation was part of the natural landscape. And as much as I hate to admit it, we took these dear older friends for granted, ignoring life's ticking clock. So it is all the more shocking and sad when one of them passes away.

With each departure, a hush falls over the lake like the last waves from a boat's wake rolling up on a quiet shore.

Lucky for us, several of these older friends have lived well into their eighties and nineties, keeping the proverbial campfire burning not only for our generation but also for the younger one behind us. Because all age groups are included in our lake activities—cabin parties, picnics, boat outings, star gazing—our children love and admire them as much as we do.

With each passing year, the few friends that are left from this generation seem more and more like national treasures. Bill and Ginny are the only couple left. Bill first came to the lake in 1929 as a young boy, and Ginny joined him as his war bride during the 1940s. They have been icons of the area ever since. Married for over sixty-seven years, they now spend their winters in Florida, but with the help of good lake friends and family, and by sheer will and determination, they return to their beloved cabin each summer. It is a thrill when we hear they've made it back. For although both are in their nineties and are battling a number of health issues, their positive spirits, humor, and charm continue to delight us at every cabin gathering or supper club outing.

In the backs of our minds, we can't help but wonder if this year will be their last, and no doubt so do they. Every time we boat by their cabin on the hill, whether or not we can see them behind the windows in their favorite porch chairs, we always honk the boat horn and offer up a big wave. More often than not, they respond by waving exuberantly or flicking their porch light in the dusk to let us know they are there.

When a recent summer came to its usual too-sudden end, underscored by the first hints of autumn's red and yellow leaves, I baked some cookies and went to see Bill and Ginny before they headed back to Florida. They offered me a chair between them on their porch with its beautiful view of the lake and its pine-studded islands. No wonder they liked to sit there into the long hours of twilight.

Although we had a good chat, there were several moments of quiet when the three of us, lined up in a row like eagles on a branch, just sat in silence, staring out at the wild glory of the lake. At the prospect of saying farewell, we were at a loss for words. Bill had speculated earlier that rain might be coming and he was right. Suddenly, a soft shower began to pinprick the lake and the wind picked up, swirling and brushing the waters into a kaleidoscope of intricate patterns.

From our porch perch, it was mesmerizing to watch nature's drizzling splendor—its arrival a welcome distraction from the uncomfortable lack of conversation. Finally, in an effort to break the awkwardness of the lengthening silence, I voiced what we all seemed to be thinking: our time together was coming to an end.

"Isn't it amazing we've been able to enjoy all this beauty for so many years?" I asked gently.

"Oh my, yes!" Bill responded, breaking out of his peaceful reverie with gusto. "We've been so lucky!"

"It's wonderful!" Ginny added in her typical good cheer, despite advancing dementia. "Every day here is such a blessing!"

I didn't hear a trace of melancholy or sadness in their voices as I had expected, only delightful enthusiasm for the gift of the day, for this shared moment of beauty before us.

Suddenly, a glimmer of sun poked through the gray clouds, speckling the dark water and shadowy forest with golden light.

"Maybe we'll see a rainbow!" Ginny said with a smile as bright as a child's.

"It might even come down and touch our dock!" Bill teased, breaking the tension and sending all three of us into grateful laughter.

Soon after, we hugged goodbye, and with a heavy heart at another season's end, I left the sweet familiarity of their old log cabin and headed back to mine. A few scarlet leaves, shaken loose from the rain shower, slowly drifted down from above as I drove through the tunnel of trees along the worn dirt lane. Once again, I wondered if I would ever see these dear friends again. Would they make it back next year?

Would I?

Under the Milky Way

Silently, one by one, in the infinite meadows of heaven,
Blossomed the lovely stars, the forget-me-nots of the angels.
—HENRY WADSWORTH LONGFELLOW

Midnight Crossing

Tonight the lake is perfectly still. My husband and I fumble along the narrow dock with a single flashlight and carefully climb into the fishing boat. Before us the dark, smooth water sparkles with reflected starlight. It is close to midnight, and the heavens are shimmering with beauty.

We are crossing the lake to retrieve our sixteen-year-old son, who is playing cards with friends at another cabin. He has never crossed the lake alone at night, and, as his nervous parents, we decide to go down and follow him home.

We rarely go out on the lake this late at night, and we are surprised at its loveliness. As we putt slowly along, the moist air brushes gently against our faces. Above is the Big Dipper, huge and magnificent. Nearby sits Cassiopeia in regal glory.

Except for the starlight, it is pitch dark, but I know exactly where I am. In front of us looms the familiar shadow of Picnic Island, where I have shared many a fine lunch of ham sandwiches and green grapes with family and friends. Along the opposite shore, my eyes make out the well-known shapes of neighbors' cabins.

In the distance up on a hill, I see, dimly, the lights of my family's 1929 log cabin, Wake Robin. It is the one where my father spent summers, as did I, as did my children, until recently, when my husband and I bought our own cabin at the other end of the lake. By the golden glow filtering through the woods, I guess that my mother and sisters have lit the kerosene lamps on the porch. It feels strange not to be up there with them in cozy familiarity.

As we skim past the outline of my family's old dock and 1954 fishing boat, my husband turns off the motor and we glide to a stop near a tiny island just offshore. The sudden stillness surprises us. In the quiet of the lake and forest, we can almost hear our hearts beat.

Magically, from out of the woods flows the sweet sound of children's laughter. From our boat's vantage point, we can see the teenagers' silhouettes on our friends' porch, playing card games, hooting joyously at wins and losses.

Our boat's arrival signals it is time to say good night. We watch as flashlights begin to bob like blinking fireflies down the wooded path to the lake. Laughter increases as the small parade descends through the darkness and all congregate on a narrow dock.

From this merry commotion a cheerful voice emerges from the darkness.

"Marnie? Is that you?" my friend whispers.

"Hi, Mary!" I whisper back. "Thanks for having the kids over."

"We've had a blast!" she answers.

There is a familiarity to this scene. Our families, both from the same hometown in Illinois, have crossed paths on this Wisconsin lake for over thirty years. When Mary and I were teenagers, our mothers—to our amazement—let us bring along our boyfriends. Those high school sweethearts are our husbands now, and memories as strong as fishing lines weave our pasts together.

I glance back to my family's dock and see a light at its end. I know it is my sister waiting for her daughter, just as our protective parents before us did, and by the look of her flickering flashlight, I guess she is turning the pages of her star guide.

As my son starts his motor, three moms and a dad watch with eagle eyes from their separate triangular points as the two teens skirt the water's edge.

"Can I spend the night at the cabin?" my son calls out as he docks the boat.

"Is that OK, Aunt Nancy?" I call back.

"It's fine," she whispers. "There's a star shower tonight. We'll stay down and watch awhile."

We sisters signal a flashlight goodnight in the soft darkness. Heading slowly back across the lake, I remember a year ago how painful it was for me to make this move from Wake Robin, the cherished log cabin of my childhood. In buying a new cabin, I felt as if I was ending an era, deserting my siblings and mother, and depriving my children of a continuing history.

Yet the move was important to my husband, who had long dreamed of owning his own cabin and who hopes to spend some retirement years here. Having shared moments on this lake with him since my sixteenth birthday, I could not have a finer or more loving husband. It was my love for him that helped me make the crossing.

But in the beauty of this night I realize that, despite the move, we are all still connected. Love and friendship and family still light the way no matter where we are. Our move has brought not a severance of the past, but an opportunity for new beginnings and experiences to share as we journey into the future from our different points of light.

As we cross the lake under the grandeur of the midnight sky, a sense of peace, gratitude, and God's presence fills my heart. I breathe the fragrant forest air and watch the starlight's twinkling reflections on the lake. Above us the Milky Way shines like glitter across the heavens. Within it the Northern Cross sparkles, pointing the way home.

Recycled Dump Days

In the bleak midwinter, in a little hut in a Northwoods forest, sits Betty the Dump Lady. With only the crows for company, she waits patiently in this frozen, plowed clearing for the next visitor to drive up and deposit garbage.

Winter is a slow time. With the tourists long gone and the seasonal residents moved back to their city homes, business has dropped off. No flies buzz, no bees hum, no children's laughter fills the air as pop cans are launched like missiles into the recycling bin. The thermometer hovers near zero. Even the occasional bear searching for a free meal has disappeared into its den to hibernate. All is crunch-cold quiet.

Summer is a different story. The dump bustles with activity, and Betty the Dump Lady, who is the equivalent of project manager, CEO, and chairman of the board, runs a tight ship.

"Green bottles here. Tin cans over there. Stop! What's in that bag? Not in my dump!"

Betty commands her operation from an office that reflects her unique and spunky style. A six-by-six wooden shack sits in the center of the ordered garbage arena. It's festooned on the outside with bouquets of rainbow-colored plastic flowers, a smiling black-and-white plastic skunk, a huge thermometer, and a plaque with the carved-out motto "Love Grows Here."

The little hut is Betty's waiting area until the next visitor appears. Inside, there is just enough room for a radio, a hot plate, a chair with a footrest for Betty's bad leg, and a small collection of her romance novels.

When our car drives up and pulls to a dusty stop, suspense hangs in the air as we watch and wait for the screen door of the little house to swing open. With a theatrical entrance, out steps Betty the Dump Lady. Dressed in thin, loose old clothes and in her senior years, she walks with slow dignity and a slight limp over to our car to check us out.

"How ya doing?" we ask.

"Oh, not bad," she replies. "My leg's bothering me a little bit, but other than that I'm doing OK."

Her soft voice belies her commanding presence. We are all a little fearful of Betty. Once we forgot to rinse the beer bottles. She sniffed them. Back home they went. Another time we hauled in bags of seaweed from the lake, which we didn't realize we could not dump there. Same result. You don't mess with Betty's dump.

She nods with recognition as we give her our name, and she checks us off her list. Watching with eagle eyes, she follows our movements as we place our garbage in the proper bins. We are careful to follow her instructions implicitly.

Of course, recycled garbage and dump supervisors were not always part of the picture. In the days of my youth (back in the 1950s and early 1960s) during summer visits to our family's cabin, getting rid of garbage simply meant driving to the township's official dumping area, a circular dirt driveway off the main road in the woods. Tin cans, vegetable peels, and assorted refuse lay scattered amid the pines, birches, and oaks. Although an eyesore, the area was a smorgasbord for all kinds of wild critters—skunks, crows, raccoons, bears, and the occasional pair of smooching teenagers.

When we were little, my brothers and sisters and I would beg our dad to take us on an evening dump excursion in hopes of seeing a bear. My father would turn his car lights off just as we approached the dump and we'd cruise in. With a dramatic flick of the switch, his car lights flooded the area, often rewarding us with the sight of a fleeing bear's rump crashing through the woods or, equally as thrilling, two teens in hot embrace in the front seat of their parked car.

The looks of surprise on both the bears' and the teenagers' faces always sent us into riotous laughter.

Sometimes my dad would turn off the motor and lights, and we'd wait hopefully for the bear's lumbering return. In the soft night, with the windows rolled down and the warm scent of garbage drifting through the car, my siblings and I struggled to sit still in the suspenseful silence. The telling clank of tin cans in the darkness rewarded our patience. A flash of headlights re-exposed the bear browsing for baked beans or the kissing teenagers.

I never necked at the dump, though not by choice. As a young girl, a date at the dump seemed very romantic. As luck would have it, by the time I became a teenager, the environmental movement was taking shape, and the dump was moved to a new location and locked up at night. My opportunity to kiss amid the crunched cans and corncobs while watching for bears was gone. Dump dates were history.

Even so, memories of the dump continue to hold a place of honor in our family. Driving Up North in our 1959 station wagon, my parents always slowed at the dump to spot for bears no matter how arduous our 450-mile journey had been.

"The dump, the dump!!" five hot, sweaty kids shouted. The pitch of our already frenzied excitement heightened, for the dump was the cherished signal that our cabin on the lake and all the summer surprises that awaited us were minutes away.

Before the dump moved to its more environmentally correct location, my mother hauled an old stone from its premises and presented it to my brother for his birthday. Although this seemed an odd gift at the time, the rest of us are now all secretly envious of his dump rock and wish we had one. Plunked down in the middle of his garden, this ten-pound hunk of pink and gray quartz sparkles regally, especially in springtime when it is encircled by the purple, orange, and white crocuses that my mother planted years ago.

So Betty the Dump Lady is right. "Love Grows Here" rings true. Hurry, spring! Warm the wings of the iridescent black fly with your soft sunshine so its buzz may signal children's laughter, fishermen's stories, and friends' visits to a lonely lady's outpost.

As for my own teenagers necking in the dump's dreamy darkness? Thankfully, I don't think Betty would allow it.

Birdsong

The owls are hooting. Their lovely song punctuates the evening's calm just as the sun begins its slow slide past the treetops. We have been hearing them in the small woods bordering our backyard and that of our neighbor's since the middle of January.

At first, there was only one owl calling, its lonely, low hoot a soft whisper in the twilight. Within a few weeks, however, a second, higher-pitched hoot joined the first, each calling to the other from not-so-distant trees.

Sometimes they carry on for hours, hooting into the deepening night in a lovers' duet. And sometimes they sing just as the early morning light climbs up from the east in a sleepy ascent, as though they're nature's designated alarm clock.

On occasion, they hoot only briefly and then are silent. On those nights, emptiness hangs heavy in the air.

Although we have spotted them only once or twice, their hoot identifies them as great horned owls, a fact I learned from my faded *Birds of North America* field guide. Dutifully, I record this ongoing owl concerto next to the great horned owl entry, a habit learned from my grandmother, Clara Borden Oatman, who kept a bird journal spanning over fifty years of her life.

This journal has long rested on my bookshelf, but until recently I had never read it. Inspired by owl calls and curious as to what she wrote, I opened its brittle pages. The brown, crumbling cover is tied with a slim silk ribbon, yellowed with age to an antique patina. On the flowered cover, she neatly printed in fountain-pen script the journal's purpose: Bird Notes. Beginning in 1911 and carrying on until 1962, my grandmother recorded her birds with the methodology of a well-trained ornithologist. Many of the entries list the bird's description, location, and song, like this one dated April 22, 1911: "Least fly catcher. Jelkes' woods. In trees near water darting about eating insects. 4 or 5 inches long. Olive green-gray head and back, grayish yellow under. 2 bars on wings. Song a weak chirp—a little like a sparrow."

My grandmother was a good listener, and she often identified birds by their songs. Music staffs with little quarter and eighth notes are sprinkled throughout the journal to more accurately capture the sweet calls that she heard.

One of my favorite discoveries is this early entry: "Feb. 14, 1910. Heard first robin." My grandmother's tradition of celebrating the first robin of spring has continued for over ninety-five years in my family. (This year, my brother heard his first robin in January, and I heard mine on February 25.) Every year of her journal chronicles the date of the robins' return.

Significant weather observations were also a part of her documentation, as in this March 7, 1930, entry: "Blizzard—left car in Chicago on trip to see art show. Worst snow storm in winter which was mildest in 40 years."

My grandmother enjoyed gardening as well and there are many mentions of her flowers:

"April, 1931: Forsythia never so nice as this year—completely covered with bloom."

Poetry was another love, and snatches of her favorite nature poems are recorded next to bird sightings and garden notes. In

1939, she includes these "excerpts from Robert Frost, a poet of New England" (her contemporary and a rising star at the time):

> It is a blue-butterfly day here in spring,
> And with these sky-flakes down in flurry on flurry
> There is more unmixed color on the wing
> Than flowers will show for days unless they hurry.

The best discovery of all, however, is my grandmother's spare sentences marking the major events of her life and dropped between her nature observations like birdsong suddenly heard in a forest. This is not the journaling of today that attempts to decode the meaning and nuances of daily existence, but rather a succinct acceptance of life in all its diversity, the joys as well as the sorrows.

Births, deaths, illnesses, and loving moments suddenly appear among the birds and flowers and poems like shooting stars against an already heavenly night. Some even reflect the history of the times.

> 1918: Mama ill. Dying September 24.

> 1934: No snow to speak of all winter. Dusty dust storms. Awful.

> 1938: Nov. 2—My darling Erle gone. [Erle was her beloved husband.]

> 1942: Dadie in services since August 31. [Dadie was her nickname for my father, David, her only child.]

> 1944: Feb. 26—Dadie and Eleanor married! 66 degrees—lovely day!

> 1945: May—Dadie in Germany near Cologne we think.

1945: August 14—War over!! We heard the news
over the radio at 6:10. Dadie in France.

1946: July 26—Received word at cabin that Stella
passed away. 6:15. [Stella was her sister.]

1947: Dadie's Little Darling Nancy Borden born
May 25—5:25 a.m.

1950: March 11—Europe on Q. Elizabeth.

1961: April 30, Sunday—Eleanor, Nancy and
Marnie came over and wore Mama's dresses and
my wedding dress. And!!! We saw a hummingbird
in the flowering bushes.

I was amazed to discover this last entry because I remember
it clearly. The sun poured into my grandmother's elegant dining
room as Nancy (thirteen) and I (eleven) begrudgingly modeled
these long silk dresses from the late 1800s in preparation for a
community event that our mother helped organize.

On this afternoon, we wanted to be with our friends, but since
we were borrowing these dresses from my grandmother (eighty-
five) and my great Aunt Mina (ninety), our mother insisted we
model the gowns for them. Adolescent moodiness soon evapo-
rated, however, as we two young sisters became aware of the two
elderly sisters' delight at seeing these intricate gowns from their
past brought to life again. The hummingbird sighting only added
to the magic.

In 1961, a year before my grandmother died, my mother (our
Girl Scout troop leader) invited her to speak to my troop about
the joys of keeping a bird journal. We were working on a conser-
vation merit badge, and at the end of her charming presentation
she gave each scout a little brown journal with a bird stamp on
the cover and the following inscription on the first page in her

neat script: "1911–1961: Interest and happiness in identification of birds and favorite poems make my little bird book a treasure to me, as it can be to you. C.B.O."

And so it has been. I started with that journal—"1961, April 10, Blue Bird"—and moved on into my field guide with this latest addition: "March 27: Twilight. Step out on deck to hear owls and spot both of them—one just above us in the oak tree and the other a short distance through the woods. The farther one hoots and shortly thereafter the one overhead takes flight—his wingspan huge—to another tree."

How glorious is that?

Even as I've been writing this essay, I have observed at my backyard feeder the scarlet plume of a cardinal, the black and white stripes of a downy woodpecker, gray mourning doves, and the happy darting of chickadees and juncos. In addition, a pair of red-bellied woodpeckers knocking at the top of an old dead tree continues to entertain me as no technology ever could.

One day, I will go back through my grandmother's journal and count her life list of birds: cedar waxwings, phoebes, golden-crowned kinglets, Canada warblers, and indigo buntings are just the beginning.

And tonight, I will listen closely once again for the owl music to begin, not just for the gift of its ethereal beauty, but as a reminder of what all the birds bring back to us in spring: a song of life, a song of hope.

My grandmother's last entry, written just three weeks before she died at the age of eighty-six, ended on that note: "1962, March 20—snow drops just up!"

No doubt the robins were back and singing.

Child of Nature

A budding branch was my first item for Show and Tell.

As my mother and my four-year-old self headed out the door to nursery school, I remembered that it was my turn to bring a favorite toy. Running late and with two other small children in tow, my mother simply snapped off a sprig of emerging green and handed it to me.

"Take this," she said. "You can show the other children that spring is on its way."

And so I did. With a bit of trepidation amid all the dolls and trucks and cowboy guns, I shyly got up and told about my twig.

There were green buds on it and that was good because soon the buds would turn into leaves, and leaves meant summer, and summer meant ice cream, and ice cream meant that you could probably go swimming, and believe me, I was off and running like a rambling rose that stopped only when the teacher politely thanked me and asked me to sit down.

Who knew little green sprouts on a brown branch could hold a class of thirty squirming four-year-olds at attention for so long?

It was my first awareness (and perhaps my young classmates' as well) of the beauty of nature. And it has stuck with me ever since.

Thankfully, both my parents had a deep and abiding love for nature, which they passed on to my four siblings and me. Even as small children, we were taught the names of wildflowers, birds, trees, and the brilliant constellations of the night sky. By a young age, we could recognize a maple leaf from an oak; quickly identify red-winged blackbirds, blue jays, or robins; and easily point out Orion or Cassiopeia in the night sky.

As scout leaders, my parents also trained us to nurture nature. Our troops often planted trees, picked up litter on our hikes, cleaned our campsites so they were better than when we arrived, and pursued a bevy of merit badges by honing our outdoor skills.

The best part, of course, was that it was all fun. We loved running around at night looking at stars, playing in the woods, discovering toads, and building campfires to roast marshmallows. But most of all, being outside surrounded by the wild beauty of nature gave us a sense of peace and freedom that we have cherished well into adulthood. It is a pleasure I have passed on to my children, and I know they will do the same for theirs.

Unfortunately, recent research suggests that all too many children prefer to stay inside to play because, as one child puts it in *Last Child in the Woods: Saving Our Children from Nature-Deficit Disorder*, "That's where all the outlets are." The author, journalist Richard Louv, defines *nature-deficit disorder* as "the human cost of alienation from nature, among them: diminished use of senses, attention difficulties, and higher rates of physical and emotional illnesses. The disorder can be detected in individuals, families, and communities."

He goes on to say that in just one generation, the allure of TV, computers, and video games is so strong that children are hardly outside anymore, and when they are, they don't know how to entertain themselves. As a result, children today are more likely to be inactive, inattentive, and overweight than ever before.

In addition, Louv says, there is "a growing body of evidence that indicates that direct exposure to nature is essential for physical and emotional health." New studies even suggest that exposure to nature may reduce symptoms of attention-deficit/

hyperactivity disorder and "improve all children's cognitive abilities and resistance to negative stresses and depression." The research is focusing not on what is lost by lack of exposure to nature but on what is gained, or "how blessed our children can be—biologically, cognitively, and spiritually—through positive physical connection to nature."

And here we always thought we were just fooling around out in the yard.

All this new research is only confirming what the renowned conservationist Sigurd F. Olson (1899–1982) observed and predicted decades ago. He wrote book after book on the need to preserve and protect not only the vast wildernesses but also the small ones.

Even before our recent technological advancements, Olson wrote and spoke with elegant passion about the great silences of the wild, the profound beauty of the natural world, and the basic human need to experience spiritual renewal in nature.

As far back as 1946, he was writing in *National Parks Magazine*, "I have found that people go to the wilderness for many things, but the most important of these is perspective. They may think they go for the fishing or the scenery or companionship, but in reality it is something far deeper. They go to the wilderness for the good of their souls."

Of all the benefits of nature, perhaps it is this balm to the spirit that is overlooked the most in our overscheduled, fast-paced society. Who among us, especially a child, doesn't need the soothing benefits of nature's beauty? And what a tragedy it would be for a whole generation of children never to appreciate birdsong, the smell of rain-washed earth, or cumulonimbus clouds forming a mountain in the sky—because they were inside watching TV or playing on the computer.

So as the days lengthen and brighten, and singing birds return, do a child, or an adult, a favor. Grab a hand and take a walk, breathe in the fresh air, plant a tree, dig a garden, enjoy the silence, watch the clouds, or look up at the stars.

Who knows what discoveries you'll make, not only about nature but about yourselves. That's the best part. And maybe, just maybe, a child's appreciation of the sounds, sights, and scents of the natural world will bloom and grow.

After all, there's a reason Mother Earth is the star of Show and Tell.

Willie the Wolf and Other Wildlife

The howl rose loud, long, and lonely. It came from the wetlands to the north, startling me out of a dreamy sleep like a splash of cold water on my face. The sound of a second howl sent shivers up my spine.

Soon more voices joined in, their plaintive cries rising into the star-filled sky like a symphony in minor key. As a young girl lying snugly in an old metal bed on our cabin porch in northern Wisconsin, I listened to the eerie music serenade the forest and echo across the lake. And then I relaxed. After all, it was only Willie the Wolf.

My father, a natural born storyteller, named all our favorite Northwoods animals and, in doing so, launched our imaginations into the realm of the wild. Besides Willie the Wolf, there were Charlie Chipmunk, Roger Raccoon, Freddie the Fox, Blackie the Bear, Marvin Musky, and other appropriately christened critters. Because they had names, we saw the area's wildlife as our friends—creatures to be respected and admired.

"Willie the Wolf lives near the swamp," our father told us. "He likes to hang out at night with his pack of other wolf friends, and that is why he is calling them."

It made perfect sense to us.

We five siblings did not fear the wildlife or see them as things to be chased, hunted, or used for our benefit. Perhaps that is why we never took up fishing. Too personal.

Consequently, when our family was Up North, we were always on the lookout for wildlife sightings. When we caught sight of a creature, we greeted it with great fanfare. If we were in the car and one of us spotted an animal, we were instructed to shout out its position for the others' benefit: "Deer on the right!" or "Fox on the left!" And if, in your excitement, you only shouted, "There's a deer!" an entire station wagon would answer back like a Greek chorus: "Where?! Where?!"

Despite the lack of specifics, our father would immediately slam on the brakes, flinging all seven of us forward and whipping us back again as our car came to a screeching halt. This, of course, would startle the creature into such a fright that, in a flash, it was gone. You had to look fast if you wanted to see wildlife in our family.

Occasionally, however, an animal was so shocked by the crazy commotion coming from our station wagon that, for a few blissful moments, it stared back in mesmerized silence before regaining its wits and hightailing it out of there.

As if on cue, another Greek chorus would wail, "He's gone! He's gone!"

But before long, we'd be rolling along the road again, the windows down and our heads in lookout positions like sentries in Al Capone's car.

Because there were still wolves in those days, deer were less plentiful and problematic than they are now, so much so that we occasionally swung by the local deer farm just to see them up close. With outstretched hands filled with corn, we watched in wonder as wide-eyed does nuzzled our fingertips with their soft wet mouths, while shy fawns stood in the background. Their trust and beauty enthralled us.

Other favorite animals included porcupines and skunks. They provided fairly frequent sightings, happily ambling across woodland paths or deserted dirt roads with leisurely intent.

One early evening, someone in our family spotted a porcupine climbing a tall oak tree behind our cabin and shouted out the sighting. As if hearing Pavlov's bell, we kids dropped what we were doing and came running.

In my mad dash, I almost decapitated myself, such was my desire to see the porcupine perched in its spiky splendor. Running blindly in the near darkness, I hit my neck on the clothesline, which flung me backward onto the ground. The porcupine, slow mover that he is, was wisely long gone, thanks to all the clamor before I recovered.

Neck injury or no, it was worth the effort.

Of course, we loved water wildlife and never tired of watching loons dive for fish, eagles soar overhead, blue herons flap by the shore, or a family of ducks glide under our dock.

The multitude of woodland insects intrigued us as well. Daddy longlegs, june bugs, pine spiders, and dragonflies all held our fascination—unless of course, they crawled on us, in which case hysterical jerking body movements accompanied by loud screaming sent them flying or scampering away. It's a wonder they didn't die of fright.

In the summer of 1961, my older sister was about to enter ninth grade and was tasked with the science assignment, common in that era, to collect bugs and return the first day of school with all species chloroformed, identified, and mounted on a corkboard. It was right up our alley. Being in the thick of Northwoods bug country, we knew she'd get an *A* even before she started.

All of us eagerly enlisted to help. At first we thought it was great fun. It was easy to catch june bugs on the kitchen window screen as they buzzed toward the light, a dragonfly on the dock, or a daddy longlegs on the log wall. Armed with old mayonnaise jars, we'd sneak up on each doomed insect, snap down the jar, and slide the lid under.

After watching it crawl around for a while, our mother would drop in the chloroform-soaked cotton ball, and the bug would meet its demise, soon to be displayed and identified on the mounting board. Although we didn't like watching them die, we didn't feel too bad either, as there were plenty more where those came from; after all, it was in the name of science.

It wasn't until we killed the luna moth that our hearts went out of the project like air out of a balloon.

At night, we usually kept a light on over the garage door to guide us back to the cabin after an evening outing. If it was late enough, we sometimes discovered a scattering of ethereal moths gathered on the weathered wooden door, as though a midnight fairy with her own gossamer wings had painted them there in our absence.

Resting on the lamp-warmed wood and lit by the overhead lightbulb were beautiful moths in all shapes, sizes, and colors. Some were ivory, golden rosy, and dusky dark, and occasionally in their midst was the exquisite eyespotted polyphemus. The night the huge, lime-green luna moth appeared, we knew we'd hit pay dirt.

Because of the lamp's attractive light and warmth, it was easy to slip the mayonnaise jar neatly over the luna's large long-tailed wings, scoop it up with the lid, and drop in the killer cotton ball. It was not so easy to watch such beauty die. Nor was it easy to stick a pin in its still, dried-out, perfectly preserved form and mount it in a straight line with all the other insects. Although my sister returned to the start of the school year with an A+ bug collection, one of the finest her teacher had ever seen, we never collected bugs again.

Instead, we learned to love and watch them in their natural habitat. A dragonfly resting on a knee was a blessing; a daddy longlegs traversing an arm was fun and fascinating; a june bug thumping the kitchen window screen was cause for delight.

But it's been a long time since I've seen a luna moth, watched a porcupine amble up a tree, smelled a skunk, or heard a wolf howl. Because of pollution, loss of habitat, overcollecting, hunting, and outright eradication, as with the wolf, much of the wildlife we observed in the Northwoods as children has either dwindled or disappeared. For a while, even the beloved loons and eagles went into an endangered tailspin. Thankfully, through the protection efforts of many, these two species are starting to increase in numbers.

But for now, it's the howl of the wolf that I miss the most. Its midnight music lent an aura of magnificence to the woods. Even as a child lying in my bed and listening to the wolves, I could sense that their song sprang from the ancient melody of creation, that somehow we are all connected on this earth. Most importantly, I understood that their harmony was something to be treasured and preserved.

Amazingly, despite modern-day encroachment, near extinction, and the steady suburbanization of the Northwoods, the wolves are starting to make a comeback. Although I have not heard or seen them yet, others have.

Perhaps one day in the not too distant future, when my little grandchild is dozing dreamily on the cabin porch and wakes to ask what that sound is, I will say, "Don't worry. It's only Willie the Wolf. He is calling his friends to come and play."

She will nod in understanding as their beautiful music lulls her back to sleep.

In the meantime, I'm still listening for the chorus to begin.

Loon Ranger

We saw the eagle first, his white head and tail feathers backlit by the early morning light.

Kayaking along the shore of a northern Wisconsin lake, we slowed our paddles and gazed at his regal majesty perched high in the feathery boughs of a tall pine.

"There's another one!" I whispered to my husband kayaking a short distance behind me. "He's just a few branches down and to the left."

We couldn't believe our luck. Although eagles are making a comeback from their daunting decline several decades ago, it is still a thrill to see one up close and personal in the wild. To see two together was like a gift from heaven.

As we watched the eagles, they watched us, their eyes clearly focused on our progress as we drifted closer to their tree. Now we could see the alertness of their black eyes, the yellow of their beaks, the elegantly sculpted details of the brown feathers covering their powerful bodies.

As we looked up into their faces and they looked down into ours, the space between us felt sacred. To be included in the eagles' circle of sight, if only for a moment, was a rare and privileged gift, a shared spiritual connection to all God's creation that was humbling.

Then, just as we glided under their branches, the spell broke.

First one eagle lifted off, his wings wide and wonderful, and then the second one took flight in a similar display of fanned feathers, the two beating a slow song into the blue sky.

Suddenly, just when we thought the moment could not be more magical, a whoosh of wings fluttered from behind us and a third magnificent eagle flapped through the air just feet over our heads in close pursuit of the other two.

As they flew off across the lake, we sat still, savoring the moment.

But then, a sad, suspicious thought entered my mind. Why had the three eagles been together in such close proximity? Slowly, I turned and looked back at the shoreline.

My heart dropped. There lay a loon, lifeless, its white belly still whole and pure against the rocks, its black-and-white wings rocking gently with the waves, its head and neck stretched out beneath the water. I wept.

The previous night, while out on a sunset cruise on our pontoon boat, we spotted a large, dark object bobbing in the water and motored over to investigate. My whole family gasped when we saw it was a loon floating face down in the lake, its wings spread-eagled.

"Oh no!" I said. "It's a dead loon!"

In reverence, we admired its beautiful body, for once close enough to see the elegant detail of its black-and-white wings.

"Let's leave it alone," I said. And mournfully we moved away to give dignity to its death.

All of a sudden, to our surprise, the loon abruptly lifted up, its wings flapping in a desperate act to take flight over the water.

"It's alive!" we shouted.

Like Peter Pan characters clapping at Tinker Bell's revival, we watched in disbelief as the loon settled back on the water and appeared to dive under. With a hope and a prayer, we continued on our way.

But it was not to be. The eagles confirmed my suspicion.

For those who have never seen one, the loon is one of the most majestic symbols of pristine wilderness still remaining. From the uniqueness of its red eyes and the white ring around its neck to the checkerboard stripes of black-and-white feathers that cover its long, elegant body, the loon is fascinating to behold, especially when it dives underwater and pops up dozens of yards away. Those who have never heard its call have missed one of the most glorious sounds on earth. The haunting, laughing, yodeling music of a loon singing across a lake is not soon forgotten.

Sigurd F. Olson, the great conservationist, described it best: "The loons were calling, I can hear them yet, echoes rolling back from the shores and from unknown lakes across the ridges until the dusk seemed alive with their music."

For the past three summers, I have been a Loon Ranger volunteer for the Sigurd Olson Environmental Institute's LoonWatch program at Northland College in Ashland, Wisconsin. My job is to help monitor the loons' spring arrival, their numbers, their nests, their chicks, and their fall departure.

Because I am often out kayaking, sailing, or boating, it is an added delight to document my sightings. And because this is my first foray into the scientific field of observation and recording, I am fascinated by the patterns and the process.

So as a lifelong lover of loons, my discovery of the dead loon brought not only a personal sadness but also the worst possible news to record in my annual report for this continually struggling species.

According to LoonWatch, extensive research shows that direct anthropogenic factors (those caused by humans) lead to 52 percent of adult loon mortality, with ingested lead fishing sinkers and jigs being one of the primary factors. Drive-by boat collisions and lawn fertilizers that pollute the lakes also contribute to loon deaths. Much of the fishing tackle that is widely used today contains lead, which, when ingested by wildlife, causes nerve damage that atrophies neck muscles, causing loons and other waterfowl to drown. By all appearances, that is probably what happened to the loon we found.

According to the Minnesota Office of Environmental Assistance, eagles are also at risk of lead poisoning due to the ingestion of lead shot found in big game and exposure to lead fishing tackle. The Raptor Center at the University of Minnesota, which has monitored injured bald eagles for lead contamination since 1980, reports that 23 percent of its injured eagles suffer from lead poisoning.

I shuddered to think that the possible lead in the loon I found could also kill those three magnificent eagles—a quadruple wildlife homicide, so to speak. Even though the eagles had been there to feast on the loon, I felt honored to have witnessed them.

In a spirit of gratitude, I rested my paddle on the bow of my kayak and paused to give thanks for the loon's life of beautiful music and for the humans who help protect them. On eagles' wings, I sent my prayer.

Night Skies Beckon

The night sang with a sacred rhythm. Not content to watch the lunar eclipse from behind my window, I threw a ski jacket over my old pink bathrobe, stepped into some serious snow boots, pulled a too-big ski cap over my head, and walked out into the frigid night air.

A surprise of radiant splendor greeted me as the earth's shadow slid slowly across the face of the moon. High in the eastern sky, a reddish cloak of darkness inched its way across the moon's silver surface. To the south, Orion stood anchoring its domain with bold brilliance. And to the north, the handle of the Big Dipper trailed downward like leaves on a vine.

Despite the subzero temperatures, the night sky filled me with warmth. Except for the lone bark of a distant dog, all was silent. Bare tree limbs silhouetted by moonlight reached upward, as though seeking an otherworldly embrace. The night was magical.

And finally, like a slow-moving game of tag, the earth's shadow fully covered its celestial friend. As the last of its silver edge disappeared, the moon transformed into shades of burnished orange and hung like a smoldering coal against the blackness of the night.

It seemed as though a sense of eternal time permeated the darkness, as though all those across the centuries who had ever gazed skyward were linked arm and arm by the glow of that lunar light.

And just when I thought the night sky couldn't get more beautiful, a shooting star burst out of the darkness right next to the moon, its long tail glimmering like a ribbon of fiery sparks. Eventually, the cold won over and, with a last look up, I slowly made my way back inside.

Although the gift of such a theatrical night is rare, I have long been entertained by the heavens. On family vacations in northern Wisconsin, my parents would frequently lead me and my four siblings down to the dock to witness the Milky Way's river of stars and to teach us the names of the constellations. Orion, Cassiopeia, the Big and Little Dipper, the Seven Sisters, and Cygnus all became our night friends.

And if the evening yielded the blazing flights of shooting stars or the eerie upward flicker of green-glowing Northern Lights, we felt we were as near to heaven as earthlings could be.

Scouting merit badges and fifth-grade science further propelled my interest in the stars. I can still vividly recall running around a dark field with my classmates while waiting to look through the telescopes that would show us the moon's face and the rings of Saturn. One look through the scope and the universe had me hooked.

As a young girl, I was amazed to learn that ancient sailors navigated across the dark oceans with only the stars to guide them. And as I learned to know the sky myself, I understood why those early civilizations, the Native Americans, and the pioneers heading west all looked up to the stars and saw stories, how the brilliance of the night sky fueled their imaginations with poetry.

An appreciation of the night sky is a wonderful lifelong gift to a child. I hope that I have passed a love of the stars on to my children and that they will do the same for theirs.

Nowadays, people rarely look up at the night sky. Understandably, busy schedules, multiple responsibilities, and just plain fatigue get in the way. Light pollution that hazes over the heavens does not help either.

However, an annual global event called Earth Hour, when people switch off their lights for one hour on an appointed night, is taking hold. Its mission is not only to remind us of the impact of our carbon imprint on the earth but also to enable the satellites, space stations, and astronauts to witness and record the return of the earth to its natural state of darkness.

For those of us below, Earth Hour is a wonderful opportunity to look up and enjoy the beauty of the night skies without light pollution. Imagine the possibilities, especially for a child: a chance to spot the constellations, to create a story based on the stars, to discuss the phases of the moon, to pretend to be a sailor on the seas, to learn not to be afraid of the dark, or perhaps most importantly, to just sit quietly in the silence of the night.

Maybe the passage from Shakespeare's *The Merchant of Venice* says it best:

How sweet the moonlight sleeps upon this bank!
Here we will sit and let the sounds of music
Creep in our ears: soft stillness and the night
Become the touches of sweet harmony.

And maybe, by turning off the lights on any given evening, we too may awaken a new harmony with heaven's radiance. All we'll have to do is look up.

Listening for Wolves

I have been listening a long time. Over half a century to be exact. Listening decade after decade for that eerie, lonesome howl to pierce the forest. Waiting year after year with an ear turned toward the pine-studded wetlands for that magical music to rise up once more. Longing, summer after summer, for that soulful song of my youth.

Listening!

Listening in the glistening moonlight, listening at dawn's golden arrival, listening in my aging heart for the voice of the wolf to sing again.

"The call of the wild," as Jack London so aptly described the wolf's wail, has haunted me ever since I first heard wolves back in the 1950s. As children summering at our family's cabin in northern Wisconsin, my siblings and I often heard their howls as they roamed the nearby tamarack wetlands ringing the north bay of our lake.

"It's only Willie the Wolf," our father would assure the five of us. "He is calling his friends for a midnight rendezvous."

We were thrilled, mesmerized, and of course, a little scared.

"Don't be afraid," he assured us. "Wolves won't attack humans. They are only curious about you. Why, I even came face to face with a big gray wolf on a snowy winter walk up here when I was just a kid back in the 1920s."

"What did you do?" we asked in suspense.

"I stared at him and he stared at me, and then we both took off running in opposite directions! I don't know who was more surprised."

And so, despite the fearsome fairy tales that were fed to so many of us in our youth, the wolves never frightened us. Calling to a friend in the wilderness, howling at the beauty of the full moon on a starry night, and roaming through a winter woods all made complete sense to us.

Consequently, whenever we were fortunate enough to hear the wolves' sonorous songs piercing the twilight, we felt as though the wilderness itself was singing us a lullaby.

Almost imperceptibly, however, their howling became more and more infrequent until one summer in the early 1960s, we realized their voices had stopped altogether.

"Have you heard the wolves yet this summer, Daddy?" we asked.

"No," he answered, a sadness crossing his face, "I have not."

He said no more. He knew what we children did not: that not everyone loved the wolves as we did. Due to occasional livestock attacks, human fear, and stubborn myths, wolves were being eradicated from the Northwoods faster than one could say, "Bull's eye!"

"My father was one of those wolf hunters," a Wisconsin friend told me recently. "I remember twenty or more fresh wolf pelts strung up in a row on our barn siding to dry. He hunted them because there was a bounty on them and we needed the money." Blasting guns replaced the wolves' mournful lament, and without their singing, the forest seemed lonelier.

Thankfully, over the course of several decades, improved education and sustainable wildlife awareness have altered the wolves' death sentence, and the animals are beginning to make a comeback in some states, including Wisconsin.

Because they were listed as an endangered species and under protection of the law, their numbers grew, so much so that gradually over the last several years, reports of seeing and hearing wolves began to surface around our Northwoods lake once again.

Oh, how I longed to be one of those witnesses!

On the tenth anniversary of September 11, I happened to be on our cabin porch, the same spot where I had last heard the wolves fifty-three years earlier. Saddened by memories of the day, I decided to play my flute, something I often did on the porch as a child, and began to perform some favorite old hymns to the empty lake and forest.

I warmed up with two verses of "This Is My Father's World," and as I let my last note fade off into the woods, a song of sweet, low harmony echoed back to me.

My heartbeat quickened. Was I hearing what I thought I was? Yet, I recognized their voices immediately, as if they were long lost old friends.

Wolves!

Loud and clear, their howls issued forth from the same old Willie the Wolf wetland home of years gone by. There were at least three of them, their howls alternating and blending with each other like an encore to my flute.

Their song lasted only a minute or two, so I quickly began to play the hymn on the next page, "Joyful, Joyful, We Adore Thee." I could barely believe it—the wolves once again sang back to me! Not wanting to stop the magic, I played a third hymn. Again, the wolves performed their own discordant descant.

Intent on making this spontaneous symphony continue, I turned the page to whatever hymns were next. On came "Silent Night" and "Away in a Manger." Each time I played, the wolves followed with their own mystical version.

Finally, however, I sensed their sudden absence. Like the murmurs and applause of a satisfied audience, the only sound that greeted me was the soft wind whispering through the pines and the gently lapping waves upon the shore. The wolves had moved on.

I'm happy to report that I have heard them several times since. Just this August, sitting with my family on our old cabin porch, our after-dinner conversation was suddenly interrupted by a loud, clear chorus of wolves. Surprised by this moonlight serenade, my husband, sister, and I hurried down to the lake so that our aging ears would not miss a note.

With twinkling stars as the stage lights and a forest-rimmed lake as our amphitheater, we sat side by side in a couple of worn chairs on the dock as though we were at our own personal wolf concert. Not chancing to break the spell, we sat in utter stillness, mesmerized by the melodies floating skyward to the Milky Way.

Haunting, lyrical, rising, falling. As though in a woodland a cappella choir, each wolf wove its voice among the others'. Sometimes a soloist would take the lead, emanating a long low howl against the backup singers. Sometimes they kept a sprightly round going, each wolf entering at a different time. And sometimes they just sang to the beat of their own drums, those ancient melodies resonating into the night.

Gradually, their voices began to fade, and, in too short a time, we were left once again to a silent amphitheater. Climbing back up the old log stairs to the cabin, the three of us sensed without speaking that we had been graced with something magical.

Recently, the government allowed hunting season on the wolves to recommence in Wisconsin. We have come full circle from their near extinction to their now well-populated but controversial status. Some argue that their numbers have thinned the trophy deer, some complain that they prey on livestock, some say out of fear and loathing, "Just shoot, shovel, and shut up."

But I say, having listened to the transcendent song of the wolf, that I have heard something beyond myself, beyond the controversies of our society, even beyond understanding.

I have heard the harmony of a shared creation.

And, in doing so, I have been blessed.

Listen!

Swimming across Big Water

The lake loomed lovely and large. It sparkled and winked in the early morning light, daring me to take the plunge. I tried to ignore it, but it was no use.

Perhaps it was the fact that my husband had greeted me as the sun rose on my sixty-fifth birthday with a cheery, "Welcome to the Senior Citizen Club!" Or maybe it was because I had just bid a tearful farewell to my son, daughter-in-law, and three little granddaughters after a splendid week together at our Northwoods cabin. It could have been the knowledge that I was successfully signed up for Medicare, Social Security, and a renewed driver's license. Or maybe it was just that I needed to do something big in defiance of growing old.

I stared out at the wild beauty of the water and answered its challenge. Why not swim to an island out in the middle of the lake to celebrate turning sixty-five? It seemed just the ticket for me. And maybe someday it would serve as an inspiration for my grandchildren, particularly my five granddaughters. I had to try.

No stylish wet suit, goggles, flippers, or swim cap for this old Northwoods girl. Instead I threw on a well-worn swimsuit, clipped my gray-streaked hair to the top of my head, stepped off the shore, and waded into the water. Its cool silkiness greeted me like a strong embrace. "Refreshing!" as my family likes to say. With my husband willing to row beside me in our old aluminum fishing boat, I was off. A loon floated nearby like a welcoming escort.

Over forty-seven years ago, I earned my Life Saving and Water Safety Instructor's certificates as a physical education requirement for college. But although I am a good swimmer, I am not a long-distance swimmer. The longest I had ever swum was thirty minutes in a lap pool at home or, when up at the lake, out and back about fifty yards three times in a row. Serious swimmers would yawn.

In addition, though I love to swim, I prefer a leisurely pace utilizing the breaststroke, sidestroke, or backstroke over the more aggressive crawl that most swimmers use. After all, what's the hurry? I find swimming not only a relaxing physical exercise but also meditative. Sometimes I get my best ideas doing the sidestroke. Besides, who wants your face in the water when you can look at the clouds?

When I was a child spending summer vacations at our family's log cabin, Wake Robin, at the other end of the lake, my mother used to challenge my four siblings and me to swim to an island about three hundred yards off our dock. She would row beside us, cheering us on. Our reward was a piece of birchbark inscribed with our accomplishment and tacked to a cabin wall. We have continued the tradition with our own children; all five cousins rose to the occasion, as had their parents before them.

As I started my swim, I was reminded of those endeavors. In spirit, I was not sixty-five years old but ten. And although my siblings and I still own and use Wake Robin, my husband and I spend most of our time at the other end of the lake at our retirement cabin, purchased to accommodate our growing family. Although it would be a big stretch for me, I decided my goal should be Picnic Island, right in the middle of the 750-acre lake and between the two cabins. It seemed like a symbolic link between my youth and my new designation as Senior Citizen.

As I breaststroked away from our dock, my destination was hidden from view. I would need to round a point of land that jutted out slightly in the middle of our bowl-shaped bay before I could see the island. Amazingly, it wasn't long before I was past the closest neighbor's dock, about fifty yards out. I had never swum this far from shore, and, I have to admit, it seemed a bit daunting, especially since I wasn't even sure I could make it to Picnic Island. But with my husband rowing calmly by my side, I knew I could grab hold of the boat's gunwales and rest if I needed to. Life jackets were at the ready, or, if I was really fatigued, I could climb the old boat ladder we had thrown in at the last minute and call it a day.

Safety nets, so to speak, were in place, and as I swam on, I wondered how far my strength would take me. Who knew? Each stroke took me closer to the deepest part of our lake, on record at sixty-four feet, and not far from the island I was headed toward. Our lake is known for its great fishing, and I tried not to think of the giant muskies that roamed the deep beneath me. I was grateful my route did not have me skimming over any waving weed beds. Instead, I chose to observe the trees, the blue sky, and the landmarks I was slowly but surely passing, one by one.

Here came Candy Island on my left, a final destination I had first considered. I had never swum there, but that goal seemed too easy. On this special day, I needed a goal I was not sure I could achieve; otherwise, where was the challenge? Still, it was a thrill to glide past Candy Island and know that, yes, I could have made that one! I was glad I was pushing on; otherwise, my swim would have been over, and at this point, I felt like my adventure had just begun.

As I passed another neighbor's dock or a signature tall pine, it seemed as if each ricocheted me forward with the energy of a pinball machine. On I swam, farther and farther out.

Slowly, I closed in on Musky Point, the farthest outer peninsula of our bay, and at long last I could see my destination. Picnic

Island, with its spires of elegant red pines, site of many a fine campfire meal, was within reach. I knew I could make it.

Yet, as I eased out of the bay and entered the wide waters of the lake, a surprising change occurred. Not only did the wind and waves pick up, but I suddenly realized I felt exhilarated, not fatigued. Glancing down the lake to the far north end, I could just make out the dock of my youth. It called to me.

"I'm feeling good," I shouted up to my husband. "I think I want to try to make it to Wake Robin. It looks like I'm about halfway there."

"Better change course then," he said. "No need to go to Picnic Island."

And so, like Peter Pan, I hung a right and turned toward my home star.

As though anticipating my move, Sisters Wind and Wave greeted me with an encouraging boost, adding a bonus buoyancy and current to help me along.

Oh, such freedom!

All around me the lake sparkled in the morning light. I was far from any shore, and with no other boats around, I felt like an otter at play. Surprisingly, my strength and confidence improved with every stroke.

All this time, my husband patiently followed me in the fishing boat, its battered silver sides reflecting the morning light.

"Are you getting tired of rowing?" I asked.

"Not at all," he said. "It's pleasant out here and a beautiful day."

Actually, at my speed, he was more drifting than rowing. He should have brought a beer and tossed in a line. Is it any wonder I've been married to that man for forty-four years?

Backstroke, sidestroke, breaststroke, float. Whatever worked at the moment was my stroke of choice; there was no rhyme or reason to my pattern. Why ruin the ambiance by counting?

Sometimes it seemed I was hardly moving at all. The spire of pine I had designated as the next landmark to pass occasionally appeared to stay in the exact same place, as if I was only treading water. The brilliant white head of an eagle perched high in its branches seemed to follow my every move.

Perhaps he thought I was prey. Maybe I was.

At this point in my swim, my body seemed to go on autopilot, freeing my mind to the whims of conscience.

For some reason, faces of old friends and family showed up in happy abundance, reconnecting me to pleasant memories from the past. It was like swimming back to the watery playground of my youth, physically, mentally, and spiritually.

After a while, however, I found myself floating on my back more often, breathing more deeply of the pine-scented air. Above me the sky glowed brilliant blue. Sculpted white clouds moved over me, casting me in alternating shadow and sunshine. I couldn't help but wonder if this is what heaven looked like. Peace with my youth and peace with aging joined hands in unified harmony. And because of that, more than anything, I felt grateful. Grateful for each day of this achingly sweet life.

It took me one hour and twenty minutes to swim the mile and a half across the big water of the lake, but I did it. As I hauled my wobbly legs up the ladder of Wake Robin's dock, rather than feeling exhausted, I experienced another surprise: the liberating gift of renewal and energy. My fear of growing older moved on with the waves.

I was stronger than I thought, could go farther than I knew. Oh, youth! Why did I not know that then?

And yet, at that moment, I realized it was not too late.

Dear twilight of twinkling possibilities! Whatever stars are within my reach, let me not miss the opportunity, but hang my hopes on the brightest one in the Milky Way and sail on.

Acknowledgments

With a grateful heart, I give thanks to:

- my husband, Dave, for his endless encouragement, insight, and wisdom as my armchair editor,

- my sons, John, Bob, and Tom, for their gracious acceptance (especially after the fact) of anything I wrote about them, and for continuous, sincere interest in and good cheer for all my writing efforts,

- my daughters-in-law, Lara, Jennifer, and Rachel, for their tender and loving friendship and support,

- my sister Nancy for her "O for Awesome" proofreading and formatting skills on my original manuscript, and for my brothers, David and Tom, and my sister Mary for always being there with lots of love,

- my late father, a.k.a. Sourdough Sam, for passing on his joy of storytelling, and my late mother, Woody, for instilling a love of family history,

- my large extended family of "out-laws" for all the kindness and fun they bring to the mix,

- the Congregational Church of Batavia for the many faces of faith that have inspired me through the years,

- the entire outstanding staff at the Wisconsin Historical Society Press, especially Kathy Borkowski, Kate Thompson, Elizabeth Boone, and Kristin Gilpatrick,

- and most importantly, my wonderful editor, Elizabeth Wyckoff, for her thoughtfulness, enthusiasm, clear insight, and beautiful suggestions,

- my delightful former editors, Denise Joyce of the *Chicago Tribune* and Bob Musinski of the *Daily Herald*, for opening doors to numerous writing opportunities,

- First Writes—a fine, funny, and talented group of writers—for sharing the journey from the get-go,

- Happy Hooker Bait and Tackle Shop owners Pat and Lori Jones, for their generosity in allowing me to park my car by their air hose for long periods of time in order to use their Wi-Fi connection in the Northwoods,

- my many dear friends (you know who you are) who have given me long years of happiness, laughter, and listening hearts,

- and most notably, my cherished grandchildren, Lily, Amber, Joy, Elena, Ryan, and Alice, for continually sharing with me their inspiring creativity and enchanting love, and for sometimes choosing my first book, *Return to Wake Robin*, for their very own special Show and Tell moments at school.

About the Author

Marnie O. Mamminga was born and raised in the Chicago area. She attended the University of Illinois at Urbana–Champaign where she earned undergraduate and master's degrees in English. Over the years, Mamminga raised three sons, taught junior high and high school English, and worked as a freelance writer and columnist.

DAVE MAMMINGA

Her publishing credits include the *Chicago Tribune, Chicago Tribune Magazine, The Christian Science Monitor, Daily Herald, Detroit Free Press Magazine, Lake Superior Magazine, Midwest Prairie Review, Reader's Digest,* and several *Chicken Soup for the Soul* books.

Mamminga has presented at many writers' workshops, including the Wisconsin Writers' Institute, and often speaks at bookclubs, organizations, and events. Her first book, *Return to Wake Robin: One Cabin in the Heyday of Northwoods Resorts,* a memoir of evocative Northwoods remembrances, received a starred review in *Publishers Weekly,* was chosen by *Parade Magazine* as one of the best reads of summer 2012, and was selected by Wisconsin Public Radio for their renowned "Chapter A Day" series.